MARKETING INSTITUTIONAL MONEY MANAGEMENT SERVICES

Meeting the Needs of Today's Plan Sponsors and Corporate Treasurers

Philip Halpern

IRWIN
Professional Publishing®
Chicago • London • Singapore

ISBN 1-55738-859-8

Printed in the United States of America

BB

2 3 4 5 6 7 8 9 0

ZGraphics, Ltd.

TABLE OF CONTENTS

The decision-making process by plan sponsors has changed significantly over the years in terms of regulations, investment policy development, and the requirements of the parties responsible for managing the plans. The effect of ERISA on agent behavior is introduced.

The successful advisor must appreciate the roles and needs of the decision makers and how their perspectives may vary. Culture and personality underlie the decisions that are eventually made.

Money managers must realize that keeping existing clients is much easier than securing new clients. The top priority of firms should be to keep their clients happy. Also discussed is the importance of professionalism when the advisor faces the unfortunate event of termination.

The inevitability of evolution in the investment management business requires that money managers continually reassess opportunities. Four emerging trends are discussed.

Some final thoughts.

The Washington State Investment Board

PREFACE

When first seriously contemplating writing about marketing to plan sponsors, I was reminded of the advice given to me by Drake Beam Morin many years ago. Drake Beam is an outplacement firm with whom corporations contract on behalf of laid-off executives. I had worked for Federated Department Stores who bid me, and others, adieu after being taken over by Campeau Corporation in 1988.

Although trained in finance, I was now in the marketing business. My product was me and I was in competition with other producers in an industry with limited demand.

At the beginning of orientation, most of my "classmates" wanted to send resumes to every prospective employer in the world in order to generate the maximum number of interviews. The rationale is easy to understand: the more firms contacted, the more interviews would be created (the wonderful theory of large numbers). This logic leads to the conclusion that the more interviews obtained, the more employment contracts would be offered.

Although it made sense at first blush, this logic is wrong. As my outplacement counselors explained, marketing does not depend on the law of large numbers. Even if more interviews were generated through a scattergun approach, quite often they would not be productive. That is because the interviews generated likely would not be with the right firms or the right people. Although contacting the masses could result in positive leads, Drake Beam urged us to spend our time searching out those organizations with which a matching of interests was more likely. Mass mailings and phone calls might make us feel better, but were unlikely to find us jobs.

Drake Beam's advice was wise: first know thyself and second know thy marketplace. Only through intensive introspection and extensive market analysis should one feel confident in developing and undertaking a sales plan. Incomplete understanding of either of these two areas will result in unfocused, wasted energies. Only through introspection can comparative advantages be recognized. Only through market analysis can organizations be identified who will pay for those advantages.

Drake Beam's wisdom has served me well while building my career. Partly by design and partly by luck, my past seven professional years have been spent as a plan sponsor (with major organizations). During this period of my life, I have been the recipient of more marketing presentations than I really care to remember.

When I first entered the investment management field, I was struck by the unique culture. Norms and values pervasive in the industry have characteristics different from those experienced elsewhere in my business dealings. I relied heavily on money management firms to educate me about the industry, including portfolio managers as well as marketing professionals. I used to ask a lot of dumb questions in an attempt to learn. (I still ask dumb questions, but they seem less dumb because my current familiarity with the industry's jargon fools people.)

What quickly became evident to me was the inconsistent attitude displayed by many money managers with whom I tried to develop meaningful professional relationships. On one hand, extreme reverence was the rule; on the other hand, irreverence was also the rule. Often respect was sincere, but most of the time the sycophantic tone was so transparent as to be insulting. My mother tells me all the time how smart and wonderful

I am, but somehow those same compliments seem a little empty coming from an individual who hardly knows me.

Of course, "playing up to the customer" has been prevalent throughout history as merchants attempt to sell their wares. What is surprising is that the attitude is exactly the same even though the investment product—which is highly technical in nature—is being sold to successful, sophisticated individuals. The selling techniques often used by marketers seem no different from those used by P. T. Barnum.

What made the circus promoter successful was his uncanny ability to make the nuances of nature appear spectacular and mystical. People will be willing to pay in order to experience that sense of wonder. That wonder can be captured by the promoter of investment management products for two reasons: the *business* of producing money elicits intense emotional reactions because the product of money is a powerful stimulant, and the capital market environment in which money is produced evolves at a phenomenal pace.

Let's talk about this second factor. Change is a constant for the investment manager operating in the capital marketplace. The astute observer will recognize quickly the tautology: markets would not be markets unless there was change. New buyers and the new expectations of existing buyers interplay with new sellers and the new expectations of sellers. Successful anticipation of buyers' and competitors' future expectations will determine who will be the real "players" in the capital markets in the future.

Of course, the managers of institutional portfolios not only react to changes in the marketplace, but also influence the evolution of markets. Readers of this book may be familiar with many of the watershed events in institutional management that began with General Motors' prefunding of pension plan assets in the 1930s. Other examples, listed in rough chronological order, include:

1. The increase of institutional investors as a percentage of market capitalization and turnover.

2. Mediocre relative performance of balanced accounts and the emergence of specialty managers.

3. The passage of ERISA, focus on fiduciary responsibility, and the rise of consultants.

4. The acceptance of modern portfolio theory, the reliance on quantitative techniques, and the success of index managers.

5. The plethora of new and more complicated investment opportunities.

6. The rapid increase in corporate pension plan assets and associated proliferation of money management firms, subsequent overfundedness of plans, and decline in asset growth.

Other watershed events occurring presently can be identified:

7. The partial devolution of investment management decisions to participants through 401(k) and 457 plans.

8. The globalization of world markets.

9. The rationalization of not only corporations but the money management industry.

10. The increasing interest of institutional investors in making direct investments through private transactions.

As these events have played out, more and more public attention has been focused on the investment of benefit assets. As a consequence, decisions by institutional investors are made with much more care and due diligence. Money managers can no longer walk into the corporate treasurer's office or a public plan and be hired simply because they are nice guys.

The advisor should assume that most plan sponsors evaluate the "purchase" of a money management firm in the same manner as the money manager purchases a stock.

Professional investment advisors spend tremendous sums on research and methodologies to evaluate the pricing of securities. In analyzing companies, for example, understanding the firm's target markets, competitive advantages, and strategic positioning is key to determining fair valuation. Yet the same rigor applied to building a portfolio of companies is too often not realistically applied by the advisors in building their own market share.

Anyone who has taken an introductory marketing class has learned the four P's of marketing: product, price, place, and promotion. After the professor has finished drumming these into the student's head, it is hard to remember that marketing is much more than this. But it is.

The mistake that most companies make is to see their product in isolation. Once the business plan is in place and the products formulated, most companies rush to market. They are sure that their unique blend of experience and product will make them immediately attractive to any and all customers. They are falling into the production mentality: we can build it better so you should buy what we build. The marketing concept stresses that every transaction is an exchange that needs to be mutually satisfying to buyer and seller. If it is not, the exchange will not take place.

How, then, can the money manager increase the chances of a satisfactory exchange?

The manager needs to first step back from his or her focus on the client and begin to look at the broader environment. Classic marketing texts list the following as the main environmental factors: the economy, legal and regulatory forces, technology, competitive forces, political issues, and sociocultural influences. Managers should continually understand how these factors now impact, and will impact in the future, client/supplier relationships.

The second step taken by the money manager should be to ask and to answer the following questions:

1. Who is the target market and how is it changing? Who are the decision makers, how do they make decisions, when do they make decisions, and what motivates them?

2. What are the products desired by the target market and what are the investment advisor's competitive advantages? Are the products offered by the advisor in demand and will the same product or other products be in demand in the future?

3. Is the advisor advantageously positioned in the marketplace to offer this product? Does the marketplace perceive this position? Is the firm best organized internally to deliver the products in demand?

Although seemingly straightforward, my experience has shown that the majority of firms do not really understand what questions to ask—let alone have the ability to answer them. It is quite easy to distinguish between plan sponsors who are and who are not introspective by observing how well they communicate with their existing and potential customers. The fact is that firms, like people, do not communicate well if they do not know the essence of their soul and their place in the universe.

Russell Mason, president of Investment Management Institute, made the following commentary on marketing investment advisory services.

> It seems to me that marketing within this industry is very much driven by "herd instinct." Firms can't afford to "market walk." It's run or be trampled by the competition. Although prevalent, this philosophy is not without its downside. While we all realize how talented the people in the investment industry are, few owners have been successful at all three of what I term the key business disciplines: administration, management of the financial assets, and marketing. So, while their intentions are well meant, they have often met with difficulty keeping their "run-run" marketing running not only on the right track, but in the right direction. Those leaders who attempted to maintain control of all three during the 1980s often found themselves struggling, and occasionally falling behind the competition as the industry grew. On the other hand, most of the firms that recognized the importance of well thought out marketing and sales programs, and had the vision to dedicate the funding and experienced marketing talent to their implementation, have prospered.[1]

In support of Mr. Mason's observations, a study of leading money management firms by Charles Burkhart of Investment Counseling underscores the importance of developing a marketing plan. His research concludes that the marketing function is becoming a legitimate discipline within the money management community. As reported in *Money Management Letter*, "We are seeing more marketing people rise to the level of principals and directors in firms. It's becoming an increasingly critical position and they are making their voices heard in the industry."[2]

The linkage is clear: The more successful advisors become in marketing their products to the sophisticated plan sponsor community, the better able sponsors will be to manage their time and to improve final decisions. In turn, marketing efforts that effectively communicate desired products will reward those firms doing the selling.

This book focuses on what professional investment advisory firms can do to maximize their business development and servicing efforts.

BOOK PREVIEW

Chapter 1 presents the requirements and interpretation of ERISA, FASB, and other regulatory rules that influence the risk and return trade-offs that underlie portfolio construction. As will be discussed, these rules also impact the decision-making process characteristic of multiple agents. Just as ERISA was a catalyst for the growth of private benefit schemes, should the law or regulations change, opportunities will change.

Understanding the role and needs of the decision makers is critical for success. This is the subject of Chapter 2. The multiple agents making up the plan sponsor organization have demands and responsibilities that precipitate certain types of behavior. Some of this behavior can be generalized across most plan sponsors; others are more unique and subtle.

The major hurdles that the money manager must overcome to get hired are defined explicitly in Chapter 3. Three groups of hurdles are discussed: soft hurdles, strategic hurdles, and returns. The soft hurdles reflect the viability of the firm and the people in the marketplace. The integrity of the philosophy, strategy, and process of the investment product make up the important strategic hurdles. Finally, the last hurdle to overcome is the success of the investment product delivering its stated objective.

Advisors will go a long way toward successful marketing efforts by internalizing these hurdles as discrete challenges.

The importance of building and maintaining a supporting organization is the subject of Chapter 4. Developing a product that meets the market demand and actually *works* are prerequisites for success.

Every firm needs to start with a coherent business plan that accurately describes the goals and objectives of the organization along with a clear delineation of responsibility among the professional staff. The formulation of a business plan would be the subject of an entirely separate book, so we will not dwell at length on the subject. Suffice it to say that this task needs to be done before *and during* any serious attempts at marketing specific products.

Chapter 5 discusses the marketing strategy and the importance of integrating marketing with the investment process and overall business planning. Marketing directors are not independent agents of the firm. The investment product must be saleable and the business stable in order for the hurdles to be successfully addressed. By the same token, resources drained from the investment and business management efforts will doom the firm to failure. All gears should be running at the same speed and support one another.

The cost-benefit analysis of seven potential marketing strategies must be assessed objectively. Some work and some do not. The money manager better damn well know the difference.

Finally, rules of social etiquette in the world of institutional investing are reviewed. Principals who do not know that soup is not to be slurped and that the dessert silverware belongs at the top of the place setting quickly will be dismissed by the Emily Posts of plan sponsordom.

The formal search process is reviewed in Chapter 6. The final exam is never an open book, and there are no second chances. Examples based on real-life responses to RFP questions will be presented and critiqued from the standpoint of their effectiveness in overcoming the hurdles presented by plan sponsors. The form of the response in terms of cogency and consistency is nearly as important as the response itself.

Should the advisor be successful in meeting the first steps in the hiring process, the final presentation discussed in Chapter 7 represents the last test. Rarely will the candidate know if the final presentation is a real contest or merely a perfunctory exercise. In either case, the manager must prepare. There is little reward for the silver medalist who comes in second best.

Even when the advisor is hired, the marketing efforts must not stop. The importance of maintaining good relations is examined in Chapter 8. Plan sponsors are becoming much more systematic in establishing criteria for fulfilling the contractual obligations. Among the specific requirements discussed include Return Performance, Style Definition, Organization, Compliance, and Client Service. A comprehensive example of a monitoring policy is provided in Appendix A.

The importance of maintaining an awareness of emerging trends in the industry is discussed in Chapter 9. The world evolves quickly, and money managers must remain current in order to succeed. Four emerging trends are detailed for the reader.

Closing thoughts are provided in the final chapter.

Endnotes

1. Russell K. Mason, "Market or Go Out of Business," *Effron Report*, Year End 1993.

2. *Money Management Letter*, October 24, 1994, vol. XIX, no. 22, p. 1.

INTRODUCTION

Stephanie Olympus is hard at work as assistant treasurer at Microdot Corporation, a major corporation based in Anywhere. She is in charge of managing the investments of assets for the defined benefit and defined contribution plans at the company. She has been in the position for two years, after various stints in corporate finance and the comptroller's office. She and her assistant, Jonathan, manage the pension cash in-house. Most of the securities owned by the plans are managed by outside advisors. A large part of her responsibilities involves monitoring the performance of those managers and ensuring compliance with the investment guidelines established in the contracts.

Stephanie presents performance, capital market developments, and recommendations to an investment committee bi-monthly. Members of the committee include the chief financial officer, general counsel, and other senior managers of the firm. Investment policy and key decisions are made by the investment committee. Like 90% of companies, the board of directors has delegated fiduciary responsibilities elsewhere by designating the investment committee as the "named fiduciary." However, once per year,

Stephanie reports performance results to a sub-committee of the board in charge of overseeing company benefits.

Although she loves portfolio theory and strategy, much of Stephanie's day is spent in meetings and administration. This includes preparing reports, reviewing contracts, directing custodial activity, responding to surveys, answering questions from senior management, resolving personnel issues, assisting in the development of new benefit programs, talking to existing managers, reading voluminous amounts of mail, and answering phone calls. When time is available, Stephanie will attend seminars, discuss investment philosophy, and develop new portfolio strategies.

The plan strives to achieve top investment performance versus the peer groups and relevant benchmarks, but that goal is less important than avoiding poor returns. Stephanie knows that most performance is dictated by the asset class weights and structure of the portfolio rather than by the individual securities selected by individual advisors. The investment committee of Microdot relies on Consultant Associates for strategic investment advice and for fiduciary protection.

Stephanie has a colleague and friend across town, Bart Cascade, who manages a multibillion-dollar public plan. Bart's responsibilities are very similar to those of Stephanie. Managing relationships is perhaps even more challenging because everything that is being said and done is available for public scrutiny. In some ways, managing a public pension plan is akin to managing a public corporation with its annual reports, public relations, and other responsibilities.

Instead of an investment committee, Bart reports to a board made up of public officials, current and retired public employees, business people, and investment professionals. All of the board members are external to the day-to-day managers of the fund, and most do not have a direct stake in the pension benefit.

Understanding the organization, process, and performance of potential advisors is usually last on the list of the many things that Stephanie and Bart have to do. Their success is dependent upon how well they manage the operations, avoiding problems and maintaining good relationships. Only when in the midst of a manager search will extensive due diligence on advisors be a high priority for Stephanie and Bart. Manager searches tend to be infrequent. Money managers who wish to be hired must be prepared to present their firm in the most favorable light when those opportunities become available.

Bob Southard is Microdot's chief financial officer and chairman of his company's investment committee on benefit assets. Bob had achieved many accomplishments in accounting and corporate finance before being named CFO. Although he has amassed a large personal portfolio, Bob's knowledge of institutional investing has been gained almost entirely while serving on Micodot's investment committee.

Bob, a certified public accountant, began his career at a Big Six accounting firm before accepting the comptroller position at Microdot. Like the other senior management team members on the investment committee, Bob's current compensation is tied directly to corporate financial targets: revenue growth, ROE, and EPS.

Returns on benefit assets have a limited effect on these corporate financial measurements. Since accounting rules require a smoothing of investment returns, the actuarial assumptions are more significant determinants on the bottom line. Consequently, the yearly discussion of those assumptions is critical to the investment committee members when wearing their corporate hats.

Although the defined benefit plan is overfunded, conservative actuarial assumptions suggest that the company will be required to plan for future funding levels. The committee members hope that funding requirements do not impede their aggressive corporate capital expenditure programs.

Bob and his colleagues on the committee are diligent about reading the agenda material prepared by Stephanie prior to the meetings. When they do not read the material, it is because of the many time demands associated with running a major corporation. The committee relies significantly on the recommendations put forth by Stephanie and Consultant Associates. Some of the committee members have developed good relations with the plan's external money managers but, for the most part, do not give them much thought except when they underperform.

Last year, Bob Southard was asked by the governor to sit on the board of the state pension plan. Bob accepted. Public board meetings are scheduled monthly rather than quarterly as at Microdot. There are several reasons for this. First, policy and process decisions tend to be much more extensive and require greater discussion time. Second, the larger public board consists of 14 independent members rather than the 5 who serve on Microdot's investment committee. These members include elected officials, ex-officio members, representatives from various employee groups, and private sector executives. Unlike Microdot, where the members share similar values and financial incentives, the perspectives of the public board members can be quite different. Broader concerns from pure investment performance are a natural outgrowth of both the nonmanagement orientation of the employee representatives and the political viewpoints of the elected officials. This is the first time many of the board members have faced the responsibility of managing a large pool of assets.

Another influence on the board and its members can be identified. The legitimizing body of a public pension plan (i.e., the legislature and taxpayer) tend to take a much more active interest in the governance structure than does that of a private pension scheme (i.e., the corporate board of directors and shareholders).

Thus, George Mashburn, the retirees' elected representative, and David Bright, the state comptroller, are faced with multiple groups who take an active interest in their activities as board members. George must report back to the retirees on a regular basis and must defend the board's actions. If a publicized investment goes sour and the retirees fail to receive a cost-of-living increase, George—fairly or unfairly—will be held accountable. David, an elected official, must testify before the legislature as well as be concerned about the perception of the voting public. Yet, armed with common sense and limited technical expertise, both David and George must rely heavily on the viewpoints of the staff, consultants, and business professionals on the board.

When creating investment policy and making decisions, all the board members must use their intuition as to who to trust and who not to trust in the money management business. Stephanie, Jonathan, Bart, Bob, George and David all play important roles in the decisions of which money managers get hired.

Chapter 1

THE IMPACT OF THE REGULATORY REQUIREMENTS AND LIABILITY CONCERNS

Although no two institutions are identical, most plan sponsors have similar mandates and challenges. U.S. corporate plans operate under the Employee Retirement Security Act of 1974 (ERISA) regulations and subsequent amendments. Compliance oversight of ERISA plans in the United States comes under the purview of the Department of Labor.

ERISA outlined fiduciary standards and has served as a catalyst in the growth, governance, and investment structure of benefit plans ever since. The influence of the 1974 act has extended well beyond corporate plans, serving as a model for public and Taft-Hartley investment trusts. Other countries, like the United Kingdom after the Maxwell scandals, have increasingly adopted mandates similar to ERISA.[1]

Other regulatory bodies in the United States, in addition to the Department of Labor, include the Internal Revenue Service (IRS), the Securities and Exchange Commission (SEC), and the Financial Accounting Standards Board (FASB). IRS has a direct impact on plan design and, thus, indirectly on asset management through funding schedules. SEC regulates security transactions and such important features as the use of soft dollars.

The importance of FASB 87 and FASB 88 rules can be observed through their influence on the calculation of pension activities on corporate financial statements. The "smoothing" of pension expense combined with the role of actuarial assumptions mitigates the impact of short-term investment performance on short-term corporate performance. Consequently, the attention of corporate senior management to the pension assets may be significantly less than its commensurate size on the balance sheet.

ERISA AND THE ROLE OF AGENTS

Fiduciary requirements and associated potential liability permeate the psyche of board and committee members and should be understood by money managers. The widespread misunderstanding of ERISA fiduciary standards has many unfortunate consequences. Money managers would be wise to be sensitive to their impact on the way decisions are made.

The two fiduciary standards of "loyalty" and "standard of care" define the agency relationship. Personal liability concerns associated with being a fiduciary have stimulated trustees to hire agents who can be relied upon to perform satisfactorily and, more importantly, who will not embarrass the board. Thus, the process of decision making must be a defensible argument in view of outside criticism. Often, the decision-making process is more important than the result.

A full appreciation of the duties imposed on the fiduciary by the economic and regulatory environment cannot be realized without understanding the role of the agent. A plethora of articles and books have been circulating assessing these implications.

In a recent paper, I describe how ERISA imposes a set of requirements on corporations that may result in sub-optimal behavior.[2] The thrust of the argument lies in the multiple agency structure characteristic of most corporate benefit plans. Jensen [1989], Lakonishok et al. [1992], and others have discussed how agents may sub-optimally invest corporate assets from the interests of shareholders.[3,4]

Each layer of agent desires to transfer the accountability, if not the responsibility, of portfolio results to the next layer. Corporate officers attempt to transfer the accountability to the second layer of agents: the named fiduciaries or trustees of the fund. The trustees in turn attempt to transfer accountability to the third layer of agents: the investment advisors. One could argue that staff, as an entity separate from corporate officers, are an additional layer of agent since they may have distinct personal goals and objectives.

At each step of transference, a conservative tilt is likely to be added to the management direction given to the next agent in line. This is because each agent's career success becomes less and less tied to exceptional portfolio performance. Hence, the risk of failure becomes important. Asset allocation and external manager investment guidelines ultimately crafted by the interested parties reflect this conservative bias.

The convergence of motivations of the corporate agent and the advisor become clear: (1) as fiduciaries, not to incur personal liability, and (2) as employees or contractors, not to lose employment as a result of underperformance.

And make no bones about it: people are willing to pay for this conversion of interests, as articulated recently in *Fortune* magazine:

> The naked truth about money managers is that their usefulness goes way beyond investment help to providing other sorts of comfort. "No honest person in the business would say you're paying for performance. What you're paying for is someone to take care of you," says Louis Harvey, president of the Boston research outfit Dalbar Financial Services. That handholding comes at a steep price. NYU's Gruber and Ned Elton and Fordham's Chris Blake found that for every dollar that bond fund investors spend on fees, they get back only 20 cents in performance. "That means the service you get had better be worth 80 cents to you," says Gruber.[5]

Two anthropologists, O'Barr and Conley [1992], make an interesting observation in their recent ethnographic study of plan sponsor organizations:

> [D]ismissal of a manager is an exceedingly rare event. For example, at the fund with 21 managers, we were told that no manager had been fired for more than four years. The reports from other funds were consistent with this. In view of the competition among managers to land new institutional accounts, this is an extraordinary fact. Either the funds we

studied are remarkably—indeed, uniquely—successful in choosing managers, or they are seeing what they want to see in the quantitative evidence in order to avoid admitting a mistake and going through the burdensome process of changing managers.[6]

The advisor who understands this commonality of perspectives will be more successful in communicating the virtues of his/her wares to the corporate plan sponsor. Both parties necessarily strive to strike the correct balance between achieving credibility through good performance and the avoidance of risk.

Likely exceptions to this rule include those investment professionals still in the growth phase of their business and/or careers. An advisor trying to differentiate himself or herself may quite rationally take greater "innovative" risks. That is, the advisor has less to lose from failure with less money under management. A product or approach with a higher probability of significant excess returns (and higher probability of significant loss) may be the preferred strategy.

An astute plan sponsor will recognize that young firms are more likely to be risk takers. It also may be true that these firms will be more likely to identify innovative strategies that will add value. In any case, everything else being equal, the payoff pattern will be different between emerging and mature advisors because of their differing business risk profiles.

Similarly, plan sponsor professionals who are comfortable in their careers or who aspire for senior-level operating positions have more to fear if things blow up. However, those who view themselves as upwardly mobile within the investment management industry may take greater risks for success. This is characteristic of professionals wishing to venture out into the money management or consulting business as their next career move.

Exceptions to the conservative nature may exist for corporations who establish independent money management subsidiaries to run their benefit assets. Subsidiaries are set up for several reasons, including: (1) liability protection (although in reality this may be limited), and (2) greater autonomy from the parent. Either of these reasons suggests the possibility of a more adventurous spirit and opportunity for advisors who take larger bets.

Agents for public pension plans generally have been at least as concerned as their corporate brethren about perceived risk. Although public plans are more subject to the requirements imposed by the individual sovereignty, in practice policies are very consistent to those mandated by ERISA. With some notable exceptions, the diverse elements that comprise public boards and the need for consensus preclude the possibility of going way out on the risk spectrum in most instances.

O'Barr and Conley [1992] make some additional, relevant observations:

> Our most significant finding was that *culture* drives investment decision making in pension funds to at least as great an extent as economics or finance. . . .

> It is not an exaggeration to say that the most prominent feature of several of the fund structures is their effectiveness in shifting responsibility for decision making away from identifiable individuals. Specifically, there seems to be a roughly inverse relation in any given organization between the level of trading activity and the ability to assign individual responsibility for investment decisions. As the number of investment decisions—and, consequently, the likelihood of error—increases, so too do the complexity and consequent impenetrability of the decision-making structure.[7]

Not to overplay this theme relative to other ventures, Keith Ambachtsheer asked O'Barr and Conley at a conference if they would anticipate reaching vastly different conclusions had they chosen to study the auto, chemical, computer, or food industries rather than the pension investment industry. In short their answer was "probably not."[8]

THE IMPACT OF LIABILITIES ON ASSET MANAGEMENT

I have often joked with my colleagues that the only reason to have beneficiaries is to support our investment programs. Yet, regulatory agents, actuaries, and beneficiaries seem to insist that investment portfolio trusts are no more than prefunded vehicles established in order to pay for future committed obligations.

Of course, all kidding aside, the raison d'etre of institutional money management is the fiduciary obligation entrusted by the sponsoring organization or individual beneficiaries.

Many consultants (particularly the actuary firms) spend a great deal of time with their clients discussing the coupling of investment policy with liabilities. Almost every plan with which I am familiar goes through this exercise once every couple of years. After all, the corpus that we spend so much time investing would not exist were it not for a future financial obligation that has to be met.

Funding requirements by the regulators for less funded plans can be an important determinant of fund management style, but not in any generalizable way. Stringent accounting requirements for unfunded plans may generate one of two opposite reactions: plan sponsors may make up the shortfall and take on additional risk, or minimize the likelihood of short-term investment losses by immunizing part or all of the portfolio.

Information provided to my current employer by Wilshire Associates indicated little correlation between the fundedness of plan sponsors and their asset allocation.

Quite frankly, however, I find the extensive attention on asset-liability matching by consultants curious because plan sponsors rarely use this information due to its unclear implications. Long-term duration and inflation characteristics of most defined benefit plans would suggest a higher weighting of long-term bonds, public equity, and private equity than is commonly found.

Observed plan sponsor behavior suggests that the interplay of external environmental factors with internal cultural and personality factors, rather than individual liability requirements, determines investment structure.

CONCLUDING THOUGHTS

The economic and regulatory environments create similar opportunities and similar constraints on plan sponsor organizations. In order to mitigate any personal liability associated with fiduciary responsibility, a multiple agency structure commonly evolves, which results in the diffusion of personal benefits that might accrue to individual agents from superior performance.

Hence, conservatism and protection from failure tend to be the rule rather than the exception. The common 60% equity, 40% fixed-income allocations among pension plans reflect not so much an economic optimality as the desire to follow the crowd.

Of course, this generalization is not true of every plan. Among other factors, governance structures, risk tolerances on the part of senior management, consultant philosophy, plan history, and performance history will create different portfolio responses in the institutional marketplace. This is the subject of the next chapter.

Endnotes

1. I shall use the United States as a model in this book, but similar standards and industry evolution will increasingly parallel the American experience. Undoubtedly, the loosening of pension plan rules in other parts of the world—such as the United Kingdom, the Netherlands, Italy, Japan, Chile, and Argentina—will spawn exciting new global opportunities.

2. Philip Halpern, "ERISA and the Agency Problem: The Impact on Corporate Pension Plan Performance," *The Journal of Investing*, Fall 1993, pp. 7–16.

3. Michael C. Jensen, "Eclipse of the Public Corporation," *Harvard Business Review*, September-October 1989.

4. Josef Lakonishok, Andrei Shleifer, and Robert Vishny, "The Structure and Performance of the Money Management Industry," *Brookings Papers on Economic Activity*, 1992, pp. 339–391.

5. "The Coming Investor Revolt," *Fortune,* October 31, 1994, p. 72.

6. William M. O'Barr and John M. Conley, "Managing Relationships: The Culture of Institutional Investing," *Financial Analysts Journal,* September-October 1992, p. 26.

7. William M. O'Barr and John M. Conley, "Managing Relationships: The Culture of Institutional Investing," *Financial Analysts Journal*, September-October 1992, p. 22.

8. Keith Ambachtsheer, "Is Pension Fund Management Really Monkey Business?" *The Ambachtsheer Letter*, Toronto, Canada, November 22, 1993.

Chapter 2

UNDERSTANDING THE PLAN SPONSOR IN THE INTERNAL MARKETPLACE

O'Barr and Conley offer this somewhat unflattering description of the relationship between plan sponsors and their money managers:

> The dominant feature of the relationship between fund and manager is the illusion of control each has. Fund executives would have you believe they control the quality of their managers' work through a rigorous program of selection and evaluation. At the same time, managers talk of how they control the selection and retention processes by pandering to the ignorance and insecurities of these same executives.

> In fact, each group seems to be doing a successful job of patronizing the other, to their mutual benefit. The managers' performance typically hovers near the mean, so the fund executives are rarely embarrassed, while the managers are gainfully and profitably employed.[1]

I am not sure that I would totally agree with the extent of this illusion, but the authors are correct that both parties attempt to gain control of the relationship by pandering and cajoling the other.

Of course, their characterizations could just as easily apply to any agent who is employed to purchase products or services from vendors. By definition, agents exist because owners do not have the time, expertise, or desire to make competent decisions.

UNDERSTANDING THE PLAN SPONSOR ORIENTATION

The best way to market in diverse settings is to spend time researching and preparing how to communicate the investment theme before contacting plan sponsors. Just as companies are well researched before their stock is purchased for a portfolio, plan sponsor organizations and individuals should be well researched before the marketing call takes place.

Most institutional investors today employ some formal asset allocation process in order to craft an investment policy document. However, the money manager needs to deduce whether risk or return is the driving factor of the investment program. Although all plans may seem to have both orientations, usually one or the other dominates.

A "risk-dominated culture" tends to be very structured. Maintaining proper exposures, keeping to the target allocation, and employing various, multi-factor techniques are the key elements in this environment. Investment mangers who are successfully hired are those that add incremental return within a well-defined strategy and whose performance can be measured against a well-defined benchmark.

A "return-dominated culture" will seek out investment approaches and managers that are expected to make money. More creative and entrepreneurial investment strategies would appeal to this culture, even if the exact risks and strategic fit with the existing plan are less identifiable. If there is a gut feeling that returns will be high after normal due diligence, the sponsor is more likely to invest than its more risk-dominated brethren. In my opinion, more institutional cultures are risk-dominated rather than return-dominated

PERSONALITY TYPES

In the 1920s, Carl Jung was a pioneer in formally identifying types of personalities and the respective tendencies of thinking and functioning. Succeeding psychologists built on his work and developed more elaborate personality taxonomies. The Myers-Briggs personality tests, developed in the 1950s, have probably touched the lives of many of those now reading this page. The tests are designed to identify 16 personality types based on 4 pairs of characteristics.

To some degree, these personality types can be applied to investor groups. Communications should be tilted in a manner matching the target audience. Some basic, common sense tenets should be in the forefront of the advisor's mind when approaching individual decision makers.

Extroversion vs. Introversion

Extroverts are individuals with a strong need for sociability. They are stimulated by personal interaction (as in meetings), and the process of discourse is as important as the message itself.

By contrast, the introvert is territorial, likes space, and likes control. Meetings should be quick and to the point. The result is what counts, not the process of interaction. According to some studies, introverts account for about 25% of the population.[2]

In tailoring presentations, the advisor must determine which type the decision maker is likely to be. If an introvert, keep presentations to the point. If an extrovert, some schmoozing and storytelling may be appropriate.

Intuition vs. Sensation

The individual who has a propensity for sensation is practical; the intuitive person is likely to be more innovative. Seventy-five percent of the population describe themselves as sensation oriented.[3] The sensation-preferring individual wants facts and evidence, whether personally experienced or objectively observed. The intuitive person may reach conclusions through metaphor and imagery.

The intuitive person may be swayed by the philosophy and strategy of a particular investment style. The performance results themselves are interesting, but intuitive people will want to understand the why's and wherefore's. The sensation person may want the style to capture his or her imagination.

Quite likely, plan portfolios managed by sensation personality types are more structured and, perhaps, more passive in orientation.

Thinking vs. Feeling

Some people are more comfortable with impersonal, objective judgments and uncomfortable with personal judgments. These are thinking types. Others are more comfortable with value judgments and less with being logical and objective. These people are feeling-oriented. Individuals in our society are about evenly distributed between thinking and feeling types.[4]

The feeling person may have more visible emotional reactions and may be an easier read than the thinking person.

Advisors should be extremely focused and communicate with numbers when confronted with sensation-oriented people.

The feeling, sensation person may want to see absolute returns and make judgments accordingly. The thinking, sensation person may wish to examine the returns, but rely on formal attribution and other statistical analyses in order to assess discrete sources of return.

The feeling, intuitive individual may be more likely to take "leaps of faith" and rely on the subjective judgment that may be employed by active managers. The thinking, intuitive type may also believe that advisors can add value through active management, but will likely require more evidence before reaching any conclusion.

Judging vs. Perceiving

People who prefer closure and certainty are considered to have a judging orientation. The perceiving individual is more uncertain and less likely to feel comfortable making definitive decisions. Judging people establish deadlines and keep to them; perceiving individuals may avoid taking action. The general population is about evenly divided between the two perspectives.[5]

The difference in perspectives can be seen quite clearly by looking at the portfolio structure. Plans with many managers, particularly with similar investment mandates, clearly indicate a perceiving orientation. Judging individuals are far more likely to make significant exposure or manager bets. Perceiving plans and individuals may be far more interested in diversification and, perhaps, subject to the dangers of overdiversification.

Judging people may also hire and fire managers more quickly than their perceiving counterparts.

INVESTMENT THEMES

Clearly, the money manager should focus efforts on a plan whose orientation closely matches its competitive strengths. It would be a fascinating study to correlate Myers-Briggs personality types of decision makers with the investment themes employed in the portfolios they manage.

Some themes provide a clue to the dominant orientation of the investors:

1. Respective weights of the asset classes in the portfolio.

2. Active versus passive management in the public markets.

3. Quantitative versus fundamental investing.

4. Opportunistic investing in the public markets (e.g., emerging markets or esoteric bond products).

5. Opportunistic investing in the private markets.

Sources of Information

The money manager can derive many insights about the organizational culture and the personality of specific individuals from three general sources: written material, conferences, and personal networks.

Written sources include annual reports, press releases, articles by staff in the professional literature, and trade publication reports. The investment perspective and biases can often be gleaned quite nicely from these sources.

An additional written source that is both extremely valuable and under-utilized is a public plan request for proposals. Under most states' freedom of information acts, these are available for public use for a nominal charge.

A manager can uncover important information by examining the reports produced by one's competition: methods of better communication, investment ideas, and weaknesses to exploit. The clever manager will analyze RFP responses in order to determine which competitors succeed in the hiring process and why. I am surprised that more firms do not request RFPs as a matter of course.

Conferences provide excellent opportunities to develop contacts. However, wining and dining potential customers willy-nilly is not always the most productive use of time. The intelligent money manager will listen intently to the plan sponsor speeches and talk substantively to panelists in order to glean knowledge about where investment strategy is likely to lead. Too often, money managers listen to themselves pontificate and confuse one another's expectations with those of their clients. When at conferences, spend time listening to what people are saying rather than trying to "sell" a product.

Finally, personal networks are the most direct source of information. Meaningful relationships with plan sponsors will allow the manager to understand where the investment program is today and expectations for the future. Obviously, the best way to garner information is to speak with as many people within the targeted organization as possible. As many formal and informal interviews as possible should be an objective of the money manager looking for new business.

Conversations with connected individuals such as consultants and other plan sponsors can yield worthwhile information about targeted plans. A word of caution, however. Check and double check information because people often are misinformed. Also, because many pension decisions are made by more than one individual, there is a large element of compromise and consensus building. By the time a decision is reached, that "contact" can have been persuaded to take a slightly, or entirely, different course.

Of course, discovering information is only half of the story. The organized manager should keep extensive notes on people and organizations as news is heard. Once the effort is committed in the well-documented investment industry, money managers would be surprised how quickly a database can be established. Every piece of information about companies, plans, and individuals should be included in the money manager's database. The trick is to get into the mental habit of writing everything down and entering the information in the database immediately, indexed by both name and institution.

AREAS OF INQUIRY

From a disciplined approach to data gathering and recording, a pattern will emerge on the cultural orientation of the plan sponsor and the individuals comprising that culture. This culture has a direct impact on the investment philosophy and strategy that are employed.

The specific areas of inquiry can be articulated.

First, what is the governance structure? Who is in charge and why? The money manager must keep in mind that the default position is always the formal governance structure. At any one time strong personalities can take control but, should things go awry or the administration change, the agents of power revert to the corporate or public statute.

In the state of Washington, the legislature and individual board members took control of the Investment Board when things appeared to run amok in the late 1980s. On the corporate side in 1994, the in-house activities of the IBM pension plan were largely dismantled when senior management decided to restructure corporate operations. In both cases, and in numerous others, the formal power base reasserted control for reasons other than poor performance. However, the indirect consequence was, in the case of Washington, and likely will be, in the case of IBM, a change in investment approach.

Second, what is the historical context of the plan? Who developed the investment structure in the past, and how successful was its performance? Whether or not the program has succeeded in the past—or is perceived to have succeeded—underlies the degree of openness for change.

For example, everybody got burned in real estate, yet, everybody got burned in different markets and by different agents. Thus, a real estate advisor would be well served by understanding what failed (direct investments in-state, commingled funds managed by large institutional advisor, development property, etc.). By knowing where the sponsor got burned, the manager likely could surmise which areas the sponsor would avoid and which the sponsor would gravitate toward.

Finally, what is the orientation of the players currently in place? How do they work their own governance structure and historical context in order to achieve their goals? Who has the credibility and authority to make decisions?

In the private sector, the *de facto* decision maker is quite often the corporate pension officer. I would argue that, as long as that officer does not stray from the mandate laid out by the Committee, this situation is the most common. In some instances among the corporate plans, the consultant plays the dominant role. Be it the in-house staff or the outside consultant, many committees successfully manage an investment program by allowing the "experts" to manage the Committee. In other cases, no amount of cajoling will prevent a strong-willed CFO, treasurer, or Committee member from dominating the investment decisions.

In the public sector, a member of the staff or the consultant usually wields the most clout. However, the use of authority is less straight forward and the art of persuasion more subtle. This is because the influence and scrutiny of outside constituencies is so much greater. Also, the board members' link of financial remuneration with investment results and concomitant stock options is obviously absent on the public side. Hence, there is a greater opportunity that noneconomic goals will be asserted by board members, complicating investment decisions. Thus, one board, a subset of board members, or multiple board factions may dominate the governance process.

Most often, decision making results from a complex (and fascinating) interplay within the board and among the board, staff, and consultants. Therefore, it is important that the money manager maintain a positive dialogue with the whole panoply of individuals involved. The default position of main contact, however, should *always* be the staff member. If the manager offends the staffer, the manager is likely to be dead in the water. If the staff member is strong and desires control, it is best to back off from active participation with board members. Likewise, it is always best to maintain good relationships with consultants (as much as money managers hate these "gatekeepers").

When assessing decision making from the three inquiring perspectives just outlined, one must be careful not to confuse the formal organizational structure with the informal role playing that occurs. Confusion may occur because perceptions held by individual players may be different from one another and from reality. The more people and agents involved in decision making, the more difficulty one will have in determining the practicing governance structure. Thus, as much information as possible should be gathered and processed to develop a pattern of true decision making. If managers are not careful, misinformation will cause managers to act non-productively.[6]

Although I have no hard data, I suspect that plans that have a high turnover of board members and/or staff also have a higher level of turnover in managers. The obvious reason is that new people have new ideas. However, turnover likely indicates another phenomenon: problems with governance and consistency of investment theme. Money managers doing business with high-turnover funds, or those wishing to do business with these funds, should press their marketing efforts.

In contrast, plans that have enjoyed relatively low turnover of board and staff in the past are unlikely to exhibit turnover in the future. However, quite likely the major investment themes can be identified more easily in these plans. Thus, money managers should pursue the plans whose themes most closely parallel their own investment philosophy.

A third scenario exists when manager turnover is high while board turnover is low. Quite possibly, these funds are quicker to fire managers for underperformance. Obviously, in these cases, managers who have a consistently good track record should aggressively pursue business opportunities.

In summary, understanding the governance of the investment program, the historical context, and the current players' perspectives are the keys to developing an effective marketing plan. All three can be quite unique among plan sponsors, and recognizing the differences is critical.

Investment policy and hiring decisions result from both the common and the idiosyncratic culture. In the parlance of modern portfolio theory, the manager should strive to capture both the systematic cultural characteristics and the nonsystematic cultural characteristics.

IDENTIFYING AND UNDERSTANDING THE INDIVIDUAL DECISION MAKERS

Of course, it is too much to expect that outsiders can ascertain all of the dynamics of the decision-making process in another organization. Sometimes, even insiders have a difficult time understanding how decisions are derived in their own organization. However, I am continually amazed at money managers' poor assumptions of how decisions are made.

The statutory and corporate governance will specify the "named fiduciaries" who ultimately have responsibility for decisions. Clearly, these documents may have some value if they can be obtained. For example, corporations that designate a committee of senior managers as the named fiduciaries may suggest a higher level of day-to-day control over the fund managers than in organizations where a subcommittee of the board is the named fiduciary.

Determining the individual members' backgrounds, motivations, levels of involvement, and levels of authority are the first steps in understanding group dynamics.

Individual Backgrounds

Once the decision makers have been identified, money managers should attempt to determine backgrounds of the committee members. The make-up of the committee or board is obviously crucial. Most committees prefer unanimous decisions. For corporations, the senior managers who make up the committee may have complex relationships that cross many areas of responsibility. The management of benefit assets may be viewed as important by committee members, but likely less crucial to their career than the management of operating issues. Consequently, they may take less of a stand on the hiring or firing of investment advisors.

Thus, the level of commitment to an existing strategy or manager may be less strong. In this environment, change may be precipitated more by the staff or a limited number of committee members. On the other hand, existing relationships with the staff or leading committee member may make it harder for other money management firms attempting to break into the fold.

Turnover of committee members may also be an indication of the decision-making process. Obviously, the higher the turnover, the less expert the members. Managers who employ esoteric, complicated strategies may have less opportunity with these kinds of organizations.

With limited information and limited resources to devote to exploration, it would behoove the manager to identify the core group of individuals who have been involved the longest. Those with the historical record may set the tone and "reality" for the others. This strategy may not always work because new committee or staff members with a strong vision and persuasive personality may, over time, change the complexion of the decision-making process.

Expertise of the members is important for a number of reasons. First, if the composition of the committee members includes noninvestment professionals (e.g., human resources, operations); a conservative attitude may prevail. This may be particularly true if the corporation's legal counsel is a member. Secondly, the composition of the committee should be taken into consideration when developing presentation formats. A lower level of expertise may mean that more time needs to be spent on developing "comfort" with the organization. A higher level of expertise suggests an emphasis on investment philosophy and style.

Public plan dynamics may be even more complicated because of the visibility in the community and the various backgrounds of the board members. The composition may include some or all of the following:

- Ex-officio members (i.e., heads of state agencies). These may be political appointees or elected officials.

- Employee representatives. Although often appointed by the governor, they may also be elected by the membership group (teachers, firefighters, policemen, etc.). Also, members may represent a specific region of the state.

- Elected members from the respective houses of the legislature.

- Outside business leaders. Either the governor or the board itself may choose business leaders to serve on the board because of their management or investment expertise.

An important point that should be remembered by advisors is that the most visible and vocal board/committee members may or may not be the most influential individuals in the decision-making process. Do not be fooled by blowhards at industry conferences.

Individual Motivations

Although fiduciaries to the plan, board members may have legitimate outside perspectives that they would like to bring to the decision-making process. This may include economically targeted investments, encouragement of minority hiring practices, and so on. Attendance at board meetings might provide insight to advisors on individual member and group perspectives.

Many of the public plans have strong labor constituencies on their boards and in the legislatures that mandated their charters. This "labor" perspective may be the catalyst causing public pension plan trustees to take a less accommodating stance with senior management than that taken by traditional owners of the firm. In effect, the monitoring role by public plans against potential executive abuse of resources serves a similar function as that performed by unions. In contrast, corporate pension plan fiduciaries obviously possess a "pro-management" perspective.

Corporate responsibility and ethical behavior have been subjects of discussion for at least two decades in this country. I do not intend to pursue that topic in detail in this forum, but it is important for advisors to understand that these may not be trivial to the public pension plan board. Community activities are not a substitute for performance, but may be viewed favorably and make a difference when competing against strong competitors. Many of the board members devote their lives to public service and may volunteer their expertise to the board. Similar demonstrated sensitivity to social issues through volunteerism such as minority internships, tutoring in schools, or working on food lines at holidays, indicate a broad standard of care that can help the advisor's cause. In other words, making money need not be inconsistent with community involvement.

Individual Level of Involvement

The level of involvement of board/committee members runs the gamut from occasional participation in scheduled meetings to avariciously reading agenda material, attending conferences, perusing the literature, and meeting with managers. The activity level depends on the member's general interest in investments or interest in certain types of investments (e.g., real estate); synergy with their own careers; and other time demands.

Interestingly, I have discovered that the board/committee members' level of expertise has little to do with the level of involvement. Some of the most active members were those having the farthest to go up the learning curve. Investment is an exciting field, at least for me and for most reading this book, and it is fascinating to observe behavior following its discovery.

Not surprisingly, as people become more involved in the area, they tend to have more input into the decision-making process.

Individual Level of Authority

Authority, or influence over other committee members, is not necessarily synonymous with the level of involvement. The correlation is positive; however, the most outwardly visible members may not be the most influential within the group. The level of authority may be the most difficult to ascertain and may change depending on the particular topics for discussion.

In areas where the comfort level is low (e.g., fiduciary law, real estate financing, quantitative managers), the group will turn to committee members based on their level of expertise and level of persuasion. However, as in any group of people, some members may always sway opinions and other members may never prevail.

CONCLUDING THOUGHT

As with marketing efforts for any product, the successful firm will be one that develops keen insight into the marketplace and the customer. Some traits may be generalized; others will be specific to the plan sponsor's own governance structure, evolution, and dominant personalities.

What makes the plan sponsor particularly challenging to market toward is the speed by which the decision makers adapt to the dynamic changes taking place in the marketplace. This adaptation has resulted in plan sponsor agents becoming smarter and more demanding.

Yet, although the tests in getting hired are more strenuous today, the hurdles that the manager must overcome in order to get hired remain fairly constant. This is the subject of the next chapter.

Endnotes

1. William M. O'Barr and John M. Conley, "Managing Relationships: The Culture of Institutional Investing," *Financial Analysts Journal*, September-October 1992, pp. 26–27.

2. David Keirsey and Marilyn Bates, *Please Understand Me: Character & Temperament Types* (Del Mar, CA: Prometheus Nemesis Book Company, 1984), p. 16.

3. *Ibid.*, p. 17.

4. *Ibid.*, p. 20.

5. *Ibid.*, p. 20.

6. By way of anecdote, when the contract of the Executive Director in Washington was not renewed, many advisors informed me about what they heard on the street. Being somewhat familiar with the situation as CIO, I was quite amused at the magnitude of wrong information being bandied about on the street.

Chapter 3

INDIVIDUAL AGENTS AND THE HURDLES TO OVERCOME

Of course, it is individuals with their own highly personal views of the world that make decisions within the cultural and governance frameworks. The collective consciousness of a culture, the decision-making process, and the interactions within institutional structures mean nothing without understanding the role of individuals. Individuals both shape and are shaped by the institutions in which they serve.

Many questions should run through the mind of the money manager prior to and during personal meetings. For example, is the sponsor contact well educated or from the school of hard knocks? Extroverted or introverted? Intuitive or sensitive? Thinking or feeling? Judging or perceiving? Type A or Type B? Religious or nonreligious? Workaholic or family oriented? Broad career focus or narrow investment career focus? Developing a profile of the individual may give a clue as to which subjects to avoid and which to emphasize.

This is not to say that the manager should feign interests and beliefs in order to appear to connect with the target audience. However, the manager can attempt to identify topics of general commonality and avoid areas where different values may be present.

The fact is that, once it has been determined that the advisory candidate has the credentials and track record, the hiring decision usually comes down to a level of comfort or lack of discomfort. Can the firm be trusted? Do the principals understand what "we" need and "our" objectives? Can "we" talk to the principals? Does the investment style make sense?

In summation, if the advisor hopes to influence the judgment of decision makers, he must strive to understand the individual cultural perspectives as distinct from the larger organization and governance structure. And he must do so in a noncondescending way.

As discussed earlier, the advisor must realize that most committee and board members devote only a portion of their careers to the pension plan. Although the vast majority are committed to doing the best job possible, their personal career success rarely is affected in any significant way by investment performance of the plan. Consequently, the downside risk of underperformance and resulting bad publicity will probably hurt committee/board members' reputations more than overperformance will help. Thus, a culture of conservatism generally underlies the decision-making process.

The advisor who wishes to influence the process must appeal to this conservatism. This is true even when plan sponsors are willing to go out on a limb with a new investment approach—and many plan sponsors want to be known as being innovative in the industry even if they are by nature risk-averse. There must be some backside protection if something blows up. In reality, whether by nature or by agency demands, few plan sponsors' primary concern is not covering their backside. If things blow up, the intelligent agent will have another person or a "process" to blame.

This conservatism dictates that sponsors will be more than willing to forego the best decision for second or third best if that first choice could leave them hanging. To use statistical jargon, committee and board members will be willing to accept Type B error (not hiring the best manager) in order to avoid Type A error (hiring a bad manager).

During the decision-making process, the committee/board members establish identifiable hurdles individually and collectively that firms must overcome in order to be hired. The successful firm must overcome these hurdles in an absolute sense, but also overcome them to a sufficient degree to beat out other firms competing for the same mandate.

The remainder of this chapter's discussion will detail these hurdles. As displayed in Table 1, these hurdles can be grouped into three categories.

Soft Hurdles are hurdles of character, qualifications, and ability to serve. One can view these hurdles as the smell test before the taste. If the firm does not smell right, there is no point in taking a bite.

Strategic Hurdles are hurdles of knowledge and process. The product must meet the needs of the organization and commensurate testing standards or be eliminated from competition.

Performance is the hurdle of result. If the product has worked in the past, one might conclude it will work in the future.

TABLE 1. HURDLES FOR INVESTMENT ADVISORS TO OVERCOME

SOFT HURDLES

Hurdle 1	Credibility
Hurdle 2	Credentials
Hurdle 3	Comfort from Others
Hurdle 4	Responsiveness
Hurdle 5	Importance of Plan as a Client

STRATEGIC HURDLES

Hurdle 6	Philosophy / Style
Hurdle 7	Investment Strategy
Hurdle 8	Integrity of Investment Process

PERFORMANCE HURDLE

Hurdle 9	Returns

Money managers must remember this fact: the relative importance of each hurdle varies among the respective agents. For example, the board and committee members generally emphasize the soft hurdles while strategic hurdles often are a larger focal point among staff. Of course, individuals will scrutinize each hurdle differently. Should any single hurdle not be cleared, the firm loses its chance to play.

The process of hurdle jumping protects each agent from the ramifications of bad decisions. If the firm satisfactorily meets each hurdle and the decision still doesn't work out, the committee/board members will feel that they have performed their due diligence and cannot be criticized.

The competent staff and consultant who prescreen money management firms usually have a pretty good idea about which firms will pass the hurdles of the committee and board members, at least at a minimum level. If they are doing their jobs, each money manager will be evaluated using both their own set of standards and the perceived standard of the board and committee members: the staff and consultant won't waste the committee/board's time by selecting finalists that would fail the hurdles.

Let's now explore each hurdle in turn.

SOFT HURDLES

Hurdle 1: Credibility

In some sense, all of the hurdles are subsets of credibility, and its importance is self-evident. However, the definition of "credibility" is really difficult to pin down when examined closely. The standard of credibility is by no means consistent among agents and, when asked to define and defend, most will articulate proxies. Clearly, credibility is the softest of soft hurdles to overcome.

By credibility I mean "legitimacy." That is, the firm must prove that it is a real institutional player and not somebody who just hung up a shingle saying "Hire Me. I'll do anything with anybody for a buck."

In order to establish credibility, the manager will undoubtedly be asked (explicitly or implicitly) a set of pretty standard questions by most plan sponsors.

1. How old is the firm?

   Age establishes two things. First, whether the firm has been able to hang together through thick and thin. Having weathered the numerous seasonal changes of the financial world is in fact proof of a certain amount of mettle.

   Second, a firm with a long history indicates that it has been able to manage a business, develop products that people want to buy, and service clients. Also, a seasoned firm likely has avoided the kinds of sordid activities that have doomed their brethren—or at least they have not gotten caught. (This latter argument, of course, does not totally hold water considering recent plights of certain blueblood organizations like Barings, Prudential, and Kidder Peabody, among others).

   Age, of course, is not something one plans or can "spin." It just happens and is preferable to the only other alternative, death.

   Even this seemingly innocuous question has pitfalls. Age should not imply stodginess or hesitation to make the hard choice on the client's behalf regardless of the impact on the firm's reputation. Is the firm still hungry? Is the firm going to treat their long-standing customers better than the new customers? Different individuals may view age differently.

2. Who are the principals of the firm and are the original principals still around?

   a. How long have they been together?

   b. Have they worked in preceding organizations and, if so, what were the circumstances behind making the organizational change?

   Like the age of a firm, most people are unable to manage consciously their rate of maturation. Either the principals have been together for a while or they haven't. Almost everyone, be they board, staff, or consultant, view stable, long-lasting relationships as good things.

   Clients want to ensure that the principals will not get up and leave, and that they have stuck together through thick and thin.

3. Is the firm a household name or becoming one?

Most individuals prefer hiring a brand name rather than a generic. The Limited paid good money for the rights to the Ambercrombie & Fitch name, a bankrupt retailer whose name nonetheless had a panache still attached to it. Unless we're talking about something like Drexel or BCCI, the risk of making a mistake is perceived to be mitigated by hiring a brand-name servicer.

Although clearly a minority, some people have the opposite viewpoint. Individuals who are return-dominated rather than risk-dominated and are relatively secure in their agent role may be attracted to "yet-to-be-discovered" investment strategies and firms. Traditionally, public retirement systems in Oregon and Washington have taken big bets in private equity deals before they became legitimate asset classes for other sponsors.

4. Has the organization evolved in a manner that indicates stability and effective strategic planning?

The firm must build its organization and client base with the idea of enhancing credibility. No matter how substantive the product may be, no money manager will be able to build or to expand a book of business without effectively communicating the proxies necessary to ensure credibility to potential clients.

First, if the organization has been acquired or the outside ownership has changed, the potential client will proceed with caution. The more straightforward the ownership structure, the better. Lots of holding companies, subsidiaries, etc., might indicate a diffusion of interest and the potential for change. Internal ownership by the key professionals is viewed positively because it represents a personal stake in the firm and its products' successes. In addition to satisfying the financial incentives of the players involved, the wise firm will consider how the ownership structure will be perceived by the marketplace.

Second, the organization should be deep enough so that if any one individual leaves or is hit by a truck, management will go on relatively unchanged. Unless the product or management process is very arcane, star systems will be viewed negatively. Primary and secondary professionals should be well schooled and have had years of meaningful experience in the industry.

Third, the firm should demonstrate that its business growth has been managed so as not to impede the investment process. A strategic plan should be discussed and include a maximum number of clients and/or assets that will be accepted. An adequate explanation of why the strategic plan makes sense for the organization and product line would be desirable. Also, the firm should be structured so that portfolio managers spend the bulk of their time managing money rather than servicing clients or marketing. A breakdown of percentages spent on each activity might be helpful.

Fourth, losses should be explained honestly. Most people can understand when bad things happen, as long as there is no insidious pattern.

5. Has the firm been able to retain key personnel?

Every organization is going to incur occasional turnover of personnel for legitimate reasons. However, general stability of the professionals in the organization is a necessary, if not sufficient, condition for performance success. A productive and collegial organization where the professionals are well compensated is unlikely to have substantial turnover. A firm without a well-articulated strategic direction and where the individuals are not marching in the same direction is more likely to experience rapid turnover. Turnover is important not only because the firm has lost good people; it is also important in that it may indicate that a negative environment is taking attention away from portfolio management.

The evaluators will be looking for signals that the money managers motivate good people to stay and be productive. These signals include: promotion from within, formal career training and education programs, profit-sharing, and dispersed employee ownership structure.

If turnover has occurred, I have the following advice: fess up. An advisor who otherwise has strong qualifications could be eliminated because of a less than forthright answer regarding turnover. The industry is small and most skeletons do not reside quietly in the broom closet.

6. Has the firm or the principals been involved in any messy litigation, regulatory sanctions or investigations, or negative publicity?

Although this question is not always asked (surprisingly), the wise plan sponsor agent will want to make sure that no improprieties muck up the reputation of the prospective manager.

Potential conflicts of interest and litigation must be explained fully. Conflicts, whether real or perceived, and outstanding lawsuits are not good. However, it is better to explain the issues from the respondent's viewpoint and, again, to get everything out in the open.

7. Is the firm a known commodity on a personal level?

The reality is that, for some, credibility is gained only after years of personal relationships. Some will say that, "I don't believe what I read, numbers can lie, and education doesn't mean a damn. I don't trust anyone until I see how they operate myself." I used to be somewhat disparaging of this approach but, given the unethical behavior that sometimes exists in our business, I cannot totally discount the merits of personal experience and subjective, gut judgment.

Hurdle 2: Credentials

Credentials usually imply that the principals have the business experience and education that provide the skills necessary to do what they say they can do.

1. Have the principals achieved success in developing and implementing investment strategies?

Success means: having the creativity and stamina to develop a sound investment approach; obtaining the necessary financial support to build the required infrastructure to implement the approach; and achieving good investment performance numbers in good and bad market cycles.

2. Have the principals been leaders in the industry by demonstrating creativity and advancement?

Demonstrating creativity and advancement means being recognized by one's peers. Active participation in professional associations, speeches, and articles are all indications that the principals are plugged in to the latest technology and developments. In other words, the principals should be outward looking as well as inward looking.

Positive recognition by reputable people is observed by institutional investors in a number of ways: quotations by other professionals in presentations or articles, the winning of competitive awards or— the highest flattery of all—the copying by others of the principals' investment ideas.

3. Do solid academic and professional credentials extend down into the organization?

The breadth of the credentials among the professional investment staff obviously adds tremendously to the credibility of the firm. Hiring, training, and keeping professionals who have achieved success is extremely positive. Those of us in the business know that the interchange of ideas within the organization will mean much more to its ultimate success than the sum of the parts (as long as multiple egos do not get in the way). This also means that the organization is more likely to survive should one or two principals depart for any reason.

For most large sponsors, credentials are a necessary condition and not a sufficient condition for credibility. Credibility may mean relying solely on personal experience and gut instinct irrespective of credentials.

Hurdle 3: Comfort from Others

The sponsoring agent finds comfort in the fact that others have employed the investment approach or money manager. There are two components to this hurdle. First, being employed by others signals that the strategy is sound; their positive due diligence substantiates the sponsor's final recommendation. Acknowledged credentials and references will go a long way toward relieving the insecurity of limited technical knowledge regarding the money manager's qualifications. Second, should anything go wrong, other respected agents having made the same mistake diffuses the severity of the plan sponsor error.

1. What is the client list (i.e., does it include large, recognizable names)?

   There is no substitute for a quality client list. The status of General Motors, AT&T, CALPERS, and The Washington State Investment Board would communicate that other smart people think that the money manager is qualified.

   It is best to have this client list in the product line being marketed, although a solid client list in the firm's other product lines is almost as good.

   A recognized client list is important not just because of the "halo effect." Investors know that sophisticated plan sponsors who have solid technical and integrity reputations are invaluable sources of advice and insight to the advisor.

2. Are other clients embarking on this strategy or hiring this firm (i.e., large, recognizable clients)?

   Recent additions may be more relevant than the sum of who is on the client list. Most sponsors give the current managers the benefit of the doubt and delay termination, even if they would not hire the manager if a competitive search was held today. If the manager has experienced a recent surge in new clients (but not a deluge), this suggests that the "something special" is now being recognized.

3. Do the consulting firms recommend the firm/strategy?

   Consulting firms are investment experts and their support after extensive due diligence is reaffirming.

   Being recommended by consultants to clients, even if not finally selected, should be viewed positively. If and when appropriate, advisors might reveal the number of Fortune 500 or state pension plan finals in which they have participated, and noting the relevant consultant reference.

4. Do well known people employ similar strategies (Warren Buffet, Bill Sharpe, etc.)?

Icons of finance who tout the same methodologies, such as "small cap value" or "fundamental research," are among the best endorsements available. Using the halo effect whenever the opportunity arises usually helps and rarely hurts.

Quite honestly, some money managers believe that this hurdle is higher than it really is, or at least more important than some of the other hurdles. The vast majority of plan sponsors are confident enough of their own abilities that over emphasizing the client list implies that they are not capable of making their own decisions. Also, what the money managers cannot know is that there is sometimes antipathy toward or competition with other plans. Having them on the list could be viewed as a negative.

I am reminded of a situation several years ago when the state of Virginia and one other corporate plan embarked on a Managed Futures program. Their decisions were widely publicized in the popular press. As a result, every two days I would receive a call from a money manager engaged in this activity telling me about Virginia's decision. I said that, "This is well and good. Both the mentioned plans are respected players, but if you think that my colleagues and I are going to reprioritize our lives because of this, you've got another thing coming." I got to the point that I started getting a physical reaction when these two funds were mentioned in the Managed Futures context. Interestingly, in 1994, Virginia abandoned this program.

Hurdle 4: Responsiveness

Responsiveness is defined as the promptness, courtesy, and extensiveness with which money managers fulfill requests. Responsiveness is perhaps the most important hurdle that gets money managers into trouble, either during the search process or once hired. Unlike the other hurdles that the money manager must overcome, responsiveness is *completely* and *always* under control of the money manager. Therefore, a poor response to requests is unforgivable. I have seen and participated in the death of money manager relationships for this reason alone.

The advisor should recognize that, once hired, it is very difficult to overcommunicate. Nobody ever gets fired because of overzealous phone calls and correspondence. This is exactly the opposite of the prehiring marketing effort, when aggressive marketing can actually impede the chances of getting hired. Although correspondence may not always be diligently read by all board/committee members, the communication effort will be positively received.

When establishing the client service infrastructure, the money manager must consider not only what is convenient and expeditious for the firm but also what will most effectively meet the clients' needs and, even more importantly, how the infrastructure will be perceived by the client.

For example, regional offices may be a benefit because of time zone considerations. However, easy flights because of close proximity to the client is not a persuasive argument. The committee/board member assumes that the money manager will fly to the plan sponsor from anywhere in the world. It does not matter whether it is a 5-hour flight from New York, a 10-hour flight from London, or a 1-hour flight from Los Angeles. It may matter to the money manager, but not to the client. The client does not care how many hours the money manager travels or how many delays she endures. Also, a regional office implies a "marketing office" and the regional staff implies a "marketing staff." Marketing for new business is not perceived to be in the existing clients' interest.

Regional offices will be received positively only if time zone differences are perceived to matter and if the regional staffs are considered to be strong. Plan sponsors know that communication and consistency are not easy to maintain in a multiple-office environment.

Generally speaking, staffs/consultants are not impressed with marketing and client service people. Although many exceptions exist, client service professionals are less technically experienced and less knowledgeable in the details of the investment process. Although extremely valuable in introducing the product, once the firm is hired, these client service people can be more of a hindrance than a help—particularly if compensation is based on revenue generation rather than service. Firms that rely on dedicated client service professionals must motivate them to service the clients and to hire people who are strong facilitators. My experience suggests that the best client service professionals are those individuals who have had responsible plan sponsor staff roles or who have been portfolio managers.

1. Will extra effort be made to answer questions and to educate the board and staff?

The manager must answer all information requests—no matter how dumb or how labor-intensive—honestly, quickly, and completely. Issues that come up should be explained in great detail whether or not they are directly related to the specific mandate of the account.

The manager who is proactive in anticipating questions and issues will get many gold stars and many benefits of the doubt.

Conferences may prove a valuable tool for the money manager if they are substantive and reinforce the broader client service effort. Conferences that are set up to be boondoggles and/or substitutes for effective, ongoing communication are likely to be counterproductive and a waste of everybody's resources. I really believe that some advisors overemphasize the influence that boondoggles have on client loyalty.

2. Will resources and assistance be available to work on other investment research not directly related to managing the discretionary account?

When issues come up, be they on international economics or asset-liability matching, the manager must devote the resources to help.

3. Will the firm be supportive to the staff in its relationship with the committee/board?

In most cases, individual staff members and even committee/board members have very difficult jobs to do and have careers to build. Both objectives require manager support. The staff wants to know if the managers are going to be there when needed—can they be counted on?

As money management becomes more commodity-like in its structure, and fees decline, responsiveness will become even more crucial in manager differentiation. I am aware of one enhanced index manager who meets and exceeds all other hurdles, but who has lost business because of this failing.

Hurdle 5: Importance of Plan as a Client

The current mood of consumers everywhere seems to reflect a willingness to pay a high price for goods and services if, and only if, what is received offers high value-added and quality. Since investment advisory fees are high in both absolute terms and in relation to management salaries at the sponsoring organization, performance and service must be first-class or clients are going to be upset. This demand becomes even more strenuous because fees are ongoing and generally independent of short-term investment returns.

The fact is that once the firm is hired, the strategy agreed upon, and the securities purchased, returns will be a random event. The money manager has no control on the market prices of the securities held in the portfolio. Nor, of course, does the plan sponsor. Short of changing the investment guidelines and firing the manager, the plan sponsor has lost control of the portfolio.

The only area where the plan sponsor remains in charge is in the demand for client service. Responsiveness, as just discussed, is one major factor that must be provided by the manager. But this is only part of the equation. In the institutional marketplace, being appreciated as a customer is critical. This requirement is magnified the more idiosyncratic the investment guidelines and reporting requirements placed on the investment manager.

1. Will the principals be available at all times to answer questions?

When arguing over the best places to live, some of my friends in New York City extol the unsurpassed virtues of the cultural opportunities available there. However, when querying about how many recent plays, operas, or ballets they have attended, I am usually told few. "But we know that they are there when we get the urge."

In reality, few board or committee members will demand much time from their investment managers, but those managers must give assurances that they will be at the beck and call of this most important client.

Availability must be unquestioned during the following circumstances:

a. the annual performance review and strategy update;

b. organizational changes either at the plan sponsor or at the money manager;

c. changes in strategic or tactical direction by the plan sponsor; and

d. dramatic capital market events.

2. Will the principals attend regular meetings with the committee/board?

The trick for successful managers is to prioritize time demands. Scheduling conflicts inevitably arise for busy people with busy schedules and numerous clients. The question for the plan sponsor becomes, how high in the queue of demands will the institution be placed?

The principals better damn well make sure that the quarterly or annual (or whatever) meetings are on their schedules. When critical meetings are arranged on short notice, all else should be canceled and those meetings also attended.

3. Will the principals be managing the account or will junior portfolio managers be in charge?

Generally speaking, the reasons for hire (professional qualifications, performance, etc.) reflect the record of the principals. Plan sponsors want those principals to be the portfolio managers or, at the minimum, be on top of the accounts at all times.

I am reminded of two events in two searches. Several years ago, I was searching for a fixed-income manager to invest about $250 million. With the help of my consultant, I interviewed the important principals at several firms. I selected one firm, brought them to my committee, and they were hired. Right under my nose, the principals became less accessible and the account was transferred to a junior portfolio manager. Although somewhat guilty in not ensuring the players on my portfolio team, I was not pleased that this transfer took place. As it turned out, investment performance was good and I did not raise a big stink. But should that performance deteriorate, this firm would be given neither a lot of tolerance by me nor extra support in front of my committee. My employer was simply not that important to the firm.

The second incident was quite interesting. The Washington State Investment Board hired a manager in spite of the principals of the firm having a last-minute crisis that prevented them from attending the final presentation. The principals' expertise was clearly first-rate and I was able to allay the concerns of my board that they were qualified in spite of the absence of key players.

In a subsequent search with a differing mandate, this firm was again a finalist. Again, at the presentation, the principals were absent. This time, the board was less sympathetic and hired a different manager. I cannot honestly say that this firm would have been hired if the principals were present, but their other priority contributed greatly to their elimination.

STRATEGIC HURDLES

Hurdle 6: Philosophy/Style

The first of three strategic hurdles is investment philosophy or style. Whereas the first five hurdles largely reflect judgment and intuition, philosophy and style reflect general portfolio management tenets or rules that are necessary if the investment strategy is expected to make money.

1. Is the investment philosophy consistent with the philosophy of the board and staff members?

   Although the philosophy is sometimes difficult to pinpoint exactly, individual members who have been around awhile have developed specific perspectives. Several broad perspectives can be listed:

   a. Risk management vs. return expectations

   b. Asset-driven vs. liability-driven

   c. Active management vs. passive indexing

d. Style diversification vs. exposure diversification (i.e., is it more important to hire a mix of managers that view the world differently or a mix of managers that operate in different segments of the market?)

e. Structured/quantitative products vs. fundamental research

f. Fixed duration management vs. tactical interest-rate forecasting (i.e., for fixed-income)

g. Keeping close to policies adopted by others vs. being opportunistic

There are of course numerous other perspectives and paradigms that individuals develop over time. Depending upon each person's philosophy of the world, the individual will view the attractiveness of a manager's philosophy and style differently.

2. Can the firm articulate an overall philosophy, and do all the product lines share that common philosophy?

One of the first statements to plan sponsors should be, "This is what we believe and why. Let's get that up front and determine whether a common approach to the world exists. If yes, then there is reason for discussion. If no, then let's not waste anyone's time."

If a firm believes in value-type investing, for example, then all their products should have this theme. Otherwise, the firm will appear mercurial and create confusion in the minds of its target audience.

If the manager's philosophy and style are at odds with that of the plan sponsor, no amount of marketing or communication will be enough to overcome this hurdle. For example, I believe that it is difficult if not impossible for active large-cap managers to consistently beat the S&P 500. Several advisors who have these products to sell have spent inordinate amounts of time trying to convince me otherwise. This is silly on their part because they will never overcome Hurdle 6 with me. They would be better served by targeting plan sponsors with a different investment philosophy.

Hurdle 7: Investment Strategy

Once philosophy and style are determined to be consistent with the decision maker's own perspectives (a relatively quick hurdle to test), the investment strategy becomes the key strategic hurdle. Obviously, the investment strategy should be closely tied into the philosophy of the firm. The investment strategy is the hurdle where most of the presentation time should be spent.

1. Is the investment strategy theoretically sound?

   The investment strategy should be consistent with accepted economic theory (at least by some reputable economists), capital market behavior, etc. The manager must communicate why the strategy will work under what conditions. The reasons should be logical and tight.

   Even fundamental managers should be able to provide theoretical reasons why their approach and expertise is special. Simply saying "trust me" isn't good enough.

2. Is the investment strategy intuitive and grounded in the real world?

   Quite simply, the strategy as applied in the real world should make sense to the decision maker. Terrific-sounding rhetoric must be practical and implementable. Evidence and cogent explanations of when it works and when it doesn't, using live data, are powerful affirmations of the investment strategy.

3. Is the segment of the securities market precisely defined?

   The advisor should be crystal clear about the universe of stocks in which the firm operates. If the common consultant paradigms are appropriate (e.g., value-growth, large-small), then be explicit. If other multifactor descriptors can be identified, do so.

   On more than one occasion, I found that actual portfolio positions and results presented by managers did not reflect the universe of stocks in which the manager said they purchased. This discrepancy does not sit well with most careful readers.

4. Does the investment strategy complement the client's investment program as a whole? Does it add a new dimension to the existing asset and manager structure?

The investment strategy should fit a hole. If the plan sponsor diversifies by style, the style should vary from those employed by other investment managers. If the sponsor divides up asset classes by capitalization, value/growth, sector, etc., then the strategy should plug the missing piece.

Strategies are attractive if they provide positive alpha (i.e., positive risk-adjusted returns) with small correlation to other managers or benchmarks.

Hurdle 8: Integrity of Investment Process

The integrity of the investment process requires that the manager applies his strategy consistently and honestly. This hurdle is perhaps the most difficult for the plan sponsor to measure and for the manager to overcome.

1. Has the process been consistent over time or has it been adjusted?

Once developed, the same investment process should underlie portfolio construction through good times and bad. This is not to say that modifications should not be made with new information or research. However, significant changes to the process without clear-cut reasons will not be viewed favorably.

Situations where the investment decisions deviate from the result of the normal decision-making process should be well articulated. For example, if there is an economic or political crisis, how might the process be modified? The advisor might consider giving an example of crisis management and how the firm reacted.

The strength and discipline of the investment process ideally survives any single individual. This gets to be a little tricky. The special skill of a small number of the individuals may be the attraction of the firm; yet, the firm and investment strategy should be able to survive the departure of any key individual.

2. Has the process been tested under various market conditions?

Just as academics spend time developing hypotheses and testing their significance, investment management firms should be testing their hypothesis in a rigorous manner. Usual techniques, such as out-of-sample testing, the avoidance of data mining, etc., should be employed during the testing phase. Managers should clearly communicate the results of these tests, even to the majority of plan sponsors not well versed in econometrics.

3. Are the subject product performance results similar across client portfolios?

The manager should establish the consistency of portfolios among clients with similar objectives. A lack of consistency suggests a lack of discipline in the investment process—and the addition of another level of uncertainty.

Individual portfolio managers' expertise and discretion should be integrated with the overall investment process. Few clients would be happy if performance is the result of the luck of the draw as to which portfolio manager is assigned to the account. Even if performance is outstanding and the portfolio manager is exceptional, the "star" system is fraught with danger. The dangers lie in many directions: the star might leave, get lazy, become distracted with personal problems or other professional interests, and so on.

4. How will the evolution of the firm impact the investment process and the ability to make decisions?

As clients and asset sizes increase, the potential for market impact also increases. Using the percentage daily volume of the manager's universe of companies might be one way for the advisor to demonstrate that size would not be a foreseeable problem. Too often advisors will give an asset-dollar maximum limit of growth a little higher than the present book of business. Yet, the skeptical reader might ask whether that limit will drift up as it is approached.

Evolution that requires additional investment professionals may also impact the investment process. The advisor should address this issue straight on, emphasizing how future managers will be integrated into the philosophy and investment process employed by the firm.

5. How is the portfolio derived from a buy/sell list of individual securities?

A succinct and descriptive discussion of portfolio construction is a key, and often neglected, portion of advisor presentations. Does the advisor try to limit industry/sector exposure to the benchmark or take positions with little regard to the benchmark? Does the advisor manage factor exposures? There is no right or wrong answer, per se, since the reader may share differing, legitimate perspectives. However, the advisor must be consistent and his or her answers should reflect careful consideration.

If asked, the advisor should adequately justify the number of securities in the portfolio. In my experience, very few advisors do so. If the manager identified 40 good security ideas, are the convictions equal? If the answer is no, which generally is the case, do the portfolio weights reflect the degree of conviction?

Also, why should not the committee/board mandate the advisor to pick the best 10 or 20? Diversification, in and of itself, without specifying how diversification is measured, is a sub-par answer. The advisor should remember that the plan sponsor always has the option to achieve diversification more cheaply outside the individual active manager's account.

6. How do tailored client objectives get factored into the way investment decisions are implemented?

The advisor must walk a fine line between maintaining the consistency of implementation and the flexibility to adjust the decisions to client goals. Small deviations from normal decision making certainly can be accommodated, but large deviations suggests that the advisor is willing to compromise principle for revenue. This may come back to haunt him.

The advisor should be able to demonstrate that only those clients that adhere to the philosophy and strategy of the firm would be well served by the firm. If these do not fit a client's objectives, the advisor should refuse the business because it would be disruptive and hinder the ability of the firm to service other clients well. If the advisor can demonstrate by concrete example that they walked away from business for this reason, a substantial amount of goodwill and integrity would be conveyed. The importance of the client means that everyone is clear about objectives and the marriage will work.

As an adjunct, the advisor should review the monitoring process to assure the reader that the portfolios would always remain in compliance with the investment objectives.

7. What is your position of cash in the portfolio?

Cash in the portfolio dilutes the strength of the advisor's skill in picking stocks. Market timing should be left to the plan sponsor. If the advisor feels that their style is out-of-favor, then communicate that fact. If cash is used, it should be very infrequently and the advisor had better demonstrate that cash management skills are at least equal to those of the plan sponsor.

8. How does managing turnover and market liquidity enter into investment decisions?

High turnover is bad for several reasons. First, most people believe that excess return of individual stock securities does not occur overnight. High turnover may suggest a lack of discipline and commitment.

Second, high turnover is expensive. If turnover has been consistently high and is integral to the investment style of the manager, the client's portfolio definitely would incur a known expense while the associated payoff would be uncertain. This is a bad trade-off by any measure. Advisors who experience high turnover had best achieve outstanding results.

Addressing liquidity constraints is particularly important for large managers and/or managers who like to buy less frequently traded stocks. Proof of the advisor's sensitivity to trading costs (i.e., commissions, market impact, bid-ask spreads) should be provided. The advisor should explain any attempts to reduce costs through creative or nontraditional trading strategies.

The advisor should explain why value is added and offer proof beyond the numbers. Small cap stocks with rising earnings expectations may yield excess returns—but why? And even if the evaluators are convinced that this strategy works, what special skill does the advisor have that will allow the firm to recognize additional value added? Saying that "We're smart guys and our zillions of years of experience give us insights over and above our competition" is not a convincing argument. Also, using "proprietary" models also is not convincing. A strong, theoretical justification with objective documentation, combined with a real-life example demonstrating the investment process, would be the most convincing argument.

Just as, for example, an equity advisor looks for competitive advantages in the companies it buys, the plan sponsor is looking for competitive advantages in the advisors it hires. The exploitation of those competitive advantages should be apparent to clients when implementing the investment process.

PERFORMANCE HURDLES

Hurdle 9: Returns

Most consultants advise their clients against relying too heavily on return performance when making hiring decisions. Yet, after all the other hurdles have been cleared, the final choice between qualified firms often comes down to past return differences.

In the minds of most plan sponsors, the only "objective" number in the scoring process of searches is, of course, returns. The bottom line is the bottom line and what is a better proxy for future returns than past returns?

Of course, interpreting returns is not as simple as people make out.

1. How have the absolute returns been over short- and long-term time periods?

   Most institutional investors are astute enough to know that absolute returns mean little. However, human nature being what it is, high positive returns always make an asset class, benchmark, or investment manager look good. Gross and net returns should be spelled out for each year and, if desired, each quarter.

Risk elements are also important to many decision makers. Common measures that should be provided include, among others, standard deviations, information ratios, and Sharpe Ratios. I cannot tell you how many times these simple risk measures were not readily available.

2. How have the returns been relative to the well-known benchmarks over short- and long-term time periods?

   Relevant benchmarks should be provided by every manager in every written and oral presentation they make. Many times, managers do not provide relevant benchmarks, which implies either sloppy thinking (i.e., don't you know in what segment of the market you operate?) or deception (i.e., do you think I am so stupid as to compare a small-cap manager to an S&P benchmark?).

   Positive or negative trends against the relevant benchmarks should be explained completely and cogently.

3. Can sources of returns be identified over short- and long-term time periods?

   Many services in the industry provide attribution analytics to plan sponsors and managers. They may take the form of multivariate analysis, style analysis, sector analysis, etc. Although most systems have flaws, they do provide a valuable source of information to measure performance. These systems can also provide the manager with insight into areas that are done well and areas that are done poorly.

   Managers who proactively use these analyses and provide the results to clients communicate two positive messages. First, it indicates that the manager is willing to be forthcoming with clients. Second, it indicates that the manager is willing to spend resources to self-diagnose his or her behavior in an attempt to improve the process.

Managers should be able to answer these questions and explain returns beyond a single number. Knowing why returns have been good or poor during various periods, and communicating lessons learned, may help the manager who has less than the most stellar results win the hiring battle.

I caution the manager against playing games with returns. Playing with the time period and "equity-only" carve-outs are both obvious, tacky ploys. Also, it goes without saying that all reported returns should meet the AIMR standards.

THE ROLE AND REQUIREMENTS OF THE CONSULTANT

Before leaving this chapter, a word on the consultant is in order. Four very general roles held by the consultant can be articulated.

1. As an expert agent hired by the plan sponsor, the consultant reduces the liability of the other agents.

2. The consultant provides strategic advice on asset allocation and investment strategies.

3. The consultant measures, evaluates, and interprets investment performance.

4. The consultant assists in the selection of money management firms.

In the context of this discussion, the last role is the one of relevance. Of course, this role cannot be separated from the others. The consultant will want to reduce his own liability and protect his own business interests by not recommending any strategy or any firm that is likely to be look bad. Making a very bad recommendation is much more dangerous than not making a very good recommendation.

The consultant can be important in assisting the plan sponsor to assess the abilities of the advisor to meet the hurdles. In a recent survey published by Eager Associates, plan sponsors stated that 67% of manager searches in 1993 were conducted with the use of consultants. Interestingly, the intensity of use varied by size of the plan.

> Midsize plans—$100-250 million in assets—are at the peak. They used consultants in 78% of their searches in 1993. By contrast, plans over $5 billion in size used consultants for manager searches only 68% of the time, and for funds smaller than $100 million, the share was only 62%."[1]

The manager search business arises because of a very simple reason. The plan sponsor staff rarely has time to survey and become familiar with all the investment advisors that may be qualified to invest institutional funds. With economies of scale, an outside vendor with multiple clients is more likely to be able to afford the necessary resources to research and to develop a "buy" list of qualified firms. If the issuance of RFPs is the medium of choice, the consultant will often act as the first screen. Thus, the consultant could be viewed as acting as the referee or "gatekeeper." The size of that gate in front of the plan sponsor estate might allow many to pass, or only a few.

Unlike the portfolio manager whose performance will eventually be summed up by one number, the performance of the consultant is much more ambiguous. This is because they have no real decision-making authority: the consultant neither implements investment strategy nor contracts with money managers. Thus, the consultant is unlikely to be fired once hired, unless there are personality conflicts or the investment program is not achieving desired results.

The trade-off for job security is the relative unattractiveness of their economics compared to money management firms. Given the low-margin nature of their business, little incentive exists to intensely scrutinize new portfolio opportunities and new managers—unless the experience gained through this scrutiny can differentiate the consultant in their marketplace. Extra due diligence costs time and money.

Once a cadre of managers is available that fits the strategic niche of the consultant's clients, new managers face practical obstacles to get on the consultant's "buy" list. An incentive to carefully examine money managers may exist when there is a dearth of known competitors; otherwise, the consultant has little incentive to take the time to get to know the new firms.

There is probably no issue so misunderstood and so confusing to the money manager as the role of the consultant. This confusion arises not only because of the frustration that many managers experience in their own attempts to influence the consultant's opinion, but because of their misperceptions of the consultant's role in relation to the plan sponsor.

Having always worked with consultants in my plan sponsor role, it is amazing to me how wrong money managers can be on their perception of the consultants' relationships to their clients. In some cases, money managers believe that consultants are irrelevant to the hiring process (in spite of what they say); while in other cases staff is irrelevant and the consultant calls the shots with the Board. In more than one instance, the money managers assumed that my consultant representative was someone other than the real player and spent an inordinate amount of wasted time schmoozing the wrong person!

These misperceptions reflect the fact that consultants' roles are not consistent across plans. Based on a finite set of personal experiences, the money manager draws generalizations that will be applied toward all plans. Big mistake.

The reality is that some plans use the consultant actively and, in the extreme, may rely on the consulting agency exclusively. Other plans have no consultant. Or, in order to get several opinions, the plan may employ multiple consultants with similar mandates. The point is that myriad models for consultant use are employed in the industry.

Some committees/boards prefer that their consultant report directly to them and critique the recommendations provided by staff. These committees/boards desire to promote "dynamic tension," an often-used term, in the relationship between staff and consultant. The basis of this concept is that the best ideas will be forthcoming to the committee/board through the public argument of various positions by two antagonists.

In other cases, the consultant is "an extension of staff" and will work with staff closely in critiquing all aspects of the investment program. Good consultants under the extension of staff mandate realize that they must maintain an equal pace with regard to staff's technical requirements. The consultant works more closely with staff on a day-to-day basis and if their needs are not fulfilled, the consultant will face an obstacle in maintaining the account.

In some ways, the consultant placates his or her client by taking on the perspectives of both the committee/board and staff. The tilt that the consultant takes largely reflects the committee/board's mandate. With respect to manager search and evaluation, the direct reporting relationship requires that the consultant focus on the soft hurdles, which are less technical and more intuitive; the indirect reporting relationship through staff means that the consultant must also be diligent about assessing the strategic hurdles.

Advisors who wish to influence the consultant must emphasize both uniqueness and conformity. Product differentiation is the key to getting noticed and, with luck, getting on the buy list. However, achieving uniqueness is not useful unless the money managers perform to the strategy and paradigm employed by the consultants and their clients.

Money managers must be able to convince the consultant that their products and processes will benefit the consultant's clients. And they must sell in a manner that allows the consultant to know that the manager will meet all of the committee/board's and staff's hurdles.

Except in rare circumstances when responsibility has been delegated, meeting the consultant's screens should in no way substitute for communication efforts directed toward the hiring authority: the plan sponsors. Efforts must be doubled when the committee/ board employs the "dynamic tension" model. In this case, staff and consultant provide two distinct channels to the board rather than one.

CONCLUDING THOUGHT

Although the magnitude of importance of the hurdles varies by individual, meeting all of the hurdles is required by most decision makers. Certainly, when addressing a collection of individuals, advisors should assume that each hurdle will be a hot button for somebody.

The trick is to communicate in a manner that will be well received by people with differing personality traits, experiences, and cognitive processes.

Endnote

1. "Gatekeepers Keep Big Role in Selection," *Global Finance* (New York: Global Finance Joint Venture, January 1995), pp. 25–26.

Chapter 4

INVESTMENT PRODUCT DEVELOPMENT AND THE SUPPORTING ORGANIZATION

Developing an investment product and an organization to support delivery of that product is the subject of this very brief chapter. It is not brief because of their unimportance; it is brief because of their very great importance and the necessity of keeping this book focused.

Successful product development requires insight and intense engineering efforts. All individuals exposed to the investment industry for any length of time develop ideas of what products would sell. Some of these are generated by investment managers; some are generated by the end user and engineered in-house or through external investment advisors. I leave it to the reader to find his or her own creative investment insights. But make no mistake about it: that creativity must take place not in a vacuum but with respect to the external environment and demands, as articulated in the first two chapters.

Creating the means of production (i.e., the management organization) necessary to manufacture that product is a subject that can be taught, but it is too massive in scope for this effort. I refer the reader to books on organizational behavior or to guides such as *How to Start Your Own Money Management Business*, by Douglas K. Harman.[1]

I do feel compelled, however, to introduce this subject and to provide a perspective. As I shall argue, no marketing effort can be isolated from the investment product and the management of the organization.

PRODUCT DEVELOPMENT

The first step in product development entails defining a vision, a mission statement. For a money manager, that means creating a philosophy that can capture the imagination. The strategy takes that imagination and grounds it to the real world.

The investment philosophy and strategy must be the cornerstone of the firm and in the blood of all professional staff. The philosophy must make intuitive sense and be consistent with plan sponsors' paradigms and perceptions of reality.

Let me foray into emerging markets as an example where clear philosophy and strategy can go awry. These markets are nascent, though evolving at a rapid rate. Will quantitative approaches that rely on some stability of historical patterns make sense to plan sponsors? Probably not.

These markets also are very expensive to trade. Will active, tactical country allocation with high turnover do well in these markets? Probably not.

Combined with their rapid development, many consultants and plan sponsors have begun to view these investments in terms somewhat analogous to venture capital: real value is hard to determine, short-term prices may be overly sensitive to market manipulation and world capital market events, issues may be difficult to trade and should be valued as a long-term investment. Yet, some firms actually have marketed open-ended fund vehicles to institutional investors. Open-ended funds are structured for higher liquidity, are likely to have high turnover, and are highly sensitive to the vicissitudes of other investors' capital flows. To even a casual student of emerging markets, the associated expenses of these characteristics should far outweigh any advantages of an open-ended fund.

When the philosophy wanes or becomes less adaptive in a changing world for a previously successful firm, that firm will lose its raison d'etre. Its investment products, which result from that philosophy, will become stale.

I am reminded of an extremely successful firm that was founded by an individual (let's call him Maurice Denis) generally considered one of the founders of quantitative investment management as it exists today. For years, the success of the firm relied upon the same basic tenets and product lines that were established at the firm's origination. Yet, the technology became stale as the world changed and increasingly nimble competitors emerged. Not coincidentally, some of the bright research people had left in recent years. The firm fell behind and did not know it. Even their RFPs lacked the spark that competitors were able to generate.

Although they still possess a good book of business, the firm has won few prestigious accounts in recent years. Their investment products have lost touch with today's marketplace.

PRODUCT TESTING

My wife teaches marketing at the local college and stumbled upon a little book entitled *Marketing and Merchandising*. The text, published in 1918, is one of a series of books on modern business prepared by the editors of The Alexander Hamilton Institute in New York. The book is absolutely marvelous and most of the insights have not lost their relevance over time. This is what they have to say about product testing:

> A product is not generally pronounced ready for the market until it has been subjected to various tests. These are of two general kinds, technical tests made in the laboratory and workshop and, if the article is also of a mechanical nature, practical tests to make sure that it may be easily operated by the purchaser.

> An instance of extreme care sometimes taken is furnished in the case of Crisco, a product of the Procter and Gamble Company. This was given a series of tests lasting over a period of two years before it was accepted as a salable product. During this time it was tried out in chemical laboratories, cooking schools, private homes in different

sections of the country, restaurants, and many other places. Many changes were made in its composition as a result of the experience.

A technical test may fail, however, to do more than establish utility. It cannot tell in advance what the market will say. Only a practical tryout will settle that. For example, an attachment for a talking machine was useful and inexpensive, but did not sell. The failure was at length found to be probably due to inartistic design. The manufacturer thereupon cut away part of the metal to show an interior mechanism. This change and a wash of gold plate so improved the attachment in appearance that sales were easily made even at an advance in price.

The introduction of a new product to the market is not the only logical occasion for study and test. Machinery, package, and label designs go out of date or need freshening, for competitive reasons. The same is true of the size of the package. When war conditions forced upon American manufacturers a choice either of raising their prices or reducing the package, many chose the latter alternative. [2]

As our friends from The Alexander Hamilton Institute stated many years ago, product testing involves both proving utilitarian use and ease of operation by the purchaser. The assumptions underlying both of these must be continually evaluated and, when necessary, the product needs to be refreshed.

I encourage investment advisors to seek active counsel from their clients about product ideas, and to test their feasibility. I have developed good relations with several advisors and enjoy bantering about ideas. While many of these discussions lead nowhere, a few have led to the successful introduction of new investment products.

When introducing products to a wider marketplace, I advise managers to use the results of back-tests sparingly. Back-tests must support the strong intuition and other cogent arguments. And do not even bother reporting in-sample testing results.

THE IMPORTANCE OF THE BUSINESS PLAN

With the establishment of an investment philosophy and development of a product, the investment advisory firm must create and maintain a supporting business strategy. My first boss, a vice president of corporate planning at International Harvester in the early 1980s, once told me that strategic planning is nothing more than resource deployment.

For both a Fortune 500 company and a fledgling investment advisory firm, efficient resource deployment is required for success. The firm that effectively knows what to spend money on and what *not* to spend money on will do well. In the investment advisory business that means determining how much money is (and should be) available for staffing, training, research, computers, office space, and marketing.

Resource planning begins with a simple cash sources and uses statement. Although most entrepreneurs hate to formalize a budgeting process, the exercise is important to ensure that limited resources are deployed sequentially to areas of need (and want).

Besides establishing a base case, planning should entail various scenarios for both revenues and expenses. Every month or quarter, the principals should review the firm against the base plan and alternative scenario cases. If the firm is doing better than expected, resources could be deployed more generously. Obviously, if the firm is not doing as well, areas will have to be cut.

In talking to managers, it is absolutely shocking how even the basic planning procedures are not followed. Advisors who run their business on-the-fly do not impress diligent plan sponsors. The advisor must develop a realistic business plan in order to be competitive in today's—and tomorrow's—world of investment management.

BUILDING AND MAINTAINING
THE SUPPORTING ORGANIZATION

There is no question that building and maintaining a supporting organization for the products and the business plan must be a top priority for money managers. This is easy to say, hard to do. Establishing a good working chemistry is tough because individuals have different personalities and skill sets. Once the firm is successful at achieving this balance, maintaining stability must be a goal.

However, as technology changes and the world evolves, I have argued that the investment advisor must be nimble enough to adapt. Adaptation and stability are often at odds.

Advisory firms who become successful too fast may have the most difficult time achieving this balance. Rapid change combined with inexperience in managing complex organizational relationships can be the death of the most technically brilliant investment management company.

Recently, my board placed one of our external managers (Morisot Partners) on probation (Chapter 8 discusses the manager monitoring process and all the reasons that managers might lose good standing). Obviously, the manager was not pleased with this status and wanted to discuss the situation with me. I was able to arrange my schedule to meet for several hours in their office.

The Morisot Partners are high-quality professionals and very receptive to discussing their strengths and weaknesses. The manager has achieved a fairly good book of business. In addition, and not totally independently, the manager has had organizational change. One of the founding partners had left and, as it is a growing firm, many new junior people have been hired. Concurrent with these personnel changes, performance had dipped.

Morisot was clearly at a critical juncture of their development. For the first time in their life, growth pains seemed to take their toll. The limited number of principals were going a zillion miles a minute competing for, and winning, new accounts while, at the same time, managing a very labor-intensive portfolio. The poor performance may be a result of these growing pains and, unfortunately, the existing clients may be suffering the consequences.

Now, it is quite possible that the dip in Morisot's performance was totally unrelated to these organizational changes. However, it is very difficult to tell, given the extreme difficulty of statistically proving added value for any manager (positive or negative). As I informed the principals, my Board did not fire this manager because of this uncertainty.

I suggested that they communicate their business plan, which they have not done. How much time will the principals, who are also the key portfolio mangers, be spending on marketing, client servicing, and administration? What do they want their organization to look like? What kind of client base do they want? How do they plan to service their new clients? What value of assets under management do they desire? What new product lines are they likely to add or delete?

The partners indicated that they had spent significant amounts of time discussing these very issues and had developed a strategic plan. Yet, it did not occur to them immediately to share that strategic plan with their clients. Somehow, Morisot Partners failed to recognize the chicken and the egg: their marketing efforts created stress within the organization; that organizational stress may have affected performance; the deterioration in performance has affected the servicing of current clients, and may affect the business development efforts of future clients.

Given the intimate relationship that should develop as a result of the ongoing service and fiduciary role that advisory firms maintain with their clients, organizational stability and good organizational management by advisors are critical issues to plan sponsors. These organizational issues are as important as the investment issues: consistent, good performance cannot be achieved without efficient management.

"Eugene Boudin" is a money manager who achieved enormous success in the 1970s and early 1980s. As a contrarian manager, Boudin had no equal. He was credited with many innovations in the field and became the standard by which all active managers were judged. His innovation and creativity were renowned. The working environment for the professional staff was considered excellent.

Yet, many of the senior professionals began leaving Boudin. Of course, the consultants became concerned even though performance was still generally good. Although he was able to attract high-quality replacements because of his reputation, the turnover was viewed negatively. Why should the professionals leave Boudin? The reason seemed to be simple: Eugene Boudin was unwilling to provide equity ownership in the firm.

Eventually, performance of the U.S. product began to deteriorate. Eugene Boudin, the founder, became interested in other investment areas and seemed unconcerned about domestic results. The investment philosophy, strategy, and process for the U.S. product all evolved into something quite different. Whether this evolution was a result of new people or was a result of the lack of faith in the old ways of doing things is hard to say. Not surprisingly, consultants recommended termination and clients acted on those recommendations.

I cannot emphasize enough the importance of planning for growth by developing a realistic business plan and anticipating future needs.

Endnotes

1. Douglas K. Harman, *How to Start Your Own Money Management Business* (Burr Ridge, IL: Richard D. Irwin, Inc., 1994).

2. *Marketing and Merchandising*, volume 5 in the series Modern Business (New York: The Alexander Hamilton Institute, 1918), pp. 27–28.

Chapter 5

MARKETING STRATEGIES PRIOR TO THE FORMAL SEARCH

First, the investment advisor must understand the external industry environment (Chapter 1). Second, the advisor must ascertain how institutions have adopted internal structures and values in response to that outside environment (Chapter 2). Third, the hurdles established by the target market organizations must be understood (Chapter 3). Fourth, the advisor must develop a business plan and a product, and must establish an organization to support a product that meets the demand in the marketplace and overcomes the hurdles faced (Chapter 4). Then, and only then, is the entrepreneurial advisor ready to step in to sell his wares.

Although it sounds simplistic, few investment advisors do what it takes to discover the nuances associated with different organizations. At the very least, advisors should obtain the guidelines of the investment program and a list of current and terminated managers.

The focus of this research is to ascertain themes. For example, the money manager should determine what the target clients have done recently. Are many clients moving in one direction or another? What structure and what managers have been successful in attracting new money? Are individual consultants moving in certain directions? Are clients following their consultants' advice? Do clients have a predilection for activity vs. passivity? Value vs. growth? Fundamental vs. quantitative? Central control of managers vs. laissez-faire? High vs. low manager turnover rate?

Once the structure of the investment program is pieced together, the advisor can determine how best the firm's product fits in. Plan sponsors generally are more impressed with advisory firms who understand a broader view of the investment program's goals.

Time should not be wasted on prospects whose culture and investment structure does not mesh with the firm's product line.

WHICH IS THE REALITY AND WHICH IS THE REFLECTION: THE ADVISOR OR THE MARKETING PITCH?

In crafting a marketing strategy, firms cannot afford to be pompous, egocentric, or insincere. All verbal and written presentation material should respond to the needs and goals of the client, and demonstrate that the advisor is uniquely suited to meet those needs.

Like any business, the development of an effective marketing plan by an investment advisor is crucial to revenue growth and profitability. One could argue that marketing is even more important to a money manager than to many other types of enterprises.

When one purchases legal services, for example, attorneys who have the right academic training and have demonstrated past expertise in the needed specialty most likely will perform well for the potential client. With minimal due diligence, the client can identify these attorneys with remarkable accuracy.

Similarly, if the customer receives good service and good products at J.C. Penney, the next shopping trip to that store will most likely also be a pleasant experience. This good fortune is not a certainty, but the probability is fairly high.

However, regardless of past results, the confidence of predictive foresight for the institutional investor who hires a money management firm is not nearly so good. The benefits of working harder and smarter than the competition, as may be assumed to accrue to the best attorneys, may not be realized by the investment advisors who face the vicissitudes of the security markets. Controlling the merchandise distribution system through personal relations and pricing power, as J.C. Penney does, has little analogy to the investment advisor operating in the efficient auction market of the New York Stock Exchange. Thus, past personal experience by institutional clients or their peers is a poor proxy for future performance.

Therefore, hiring decisions really are based on subjective judgment. The only objective tool that the hiring agent possesses is the disciplined approach used to assess the *manner* by which investment advisors make investment decisions, *not the results* of those decisions.

Developing a successful marketing plan must begin with an understanding of the plan sponsor's approach to hiring evaluation. This understanding should then lead to the investment advisor building the characteristics into the firm that most likely elicits the desired results. In other words, the plan sponsor expects certain things and the investment advisor must provide them in order to be hired. Presenting a product that sells well is nearly as important as the product itself because the merits of the product are so difficult to ascertain. One could argue that, to fiduciary agents, the "look" of the product is almost as important as the product itself.

For the reader who questions this last statement, let's play a game.

Suppose you are a consultant at a major consulting firm with large institutional clients. One of your clients is doing a search for a global bond manager. You have identified three firms that have achieved good performance in the past. For ease of argument, your client only wants to interview the finalist; the Committee has chosen to rely on your judgment and the judgment of their in-house staff person.

Firm A is a subsidiary of a 200-year-old, venerable institution based in London. The Oxbridge-educated principals are articulate and meet all the hurdles discussed in Chapter 3. The English accent would go over well with the Committee members. Let's suppose that you are convinced with 80% probability that, over the long term, Firm A would meet the 100-bp risk-adjusted excess return objective of your client.

Now let's look at Firm B. The principals at Firm B are clever as hell. Their analysis and research papers have been recognized as brilliant. They have convinced you that they have identified inefficiencies in the market-place that are persistent and exploitable. Their risk-control process is disciplined, tested, and controlled. In addition, the organizational infra-structure adequately supports the firm's activities. Your analytical group has gone over the investment philosophy, strategy, and process with a fine-tooth comb and is as adamant as you have ever seen: they are 95% positive that the 100-bp risk-adjusted excess return bogey established by your client would be met by the strategy employed by Firm B.

Firm C has an outstanding marketing department. Both the principals and marketing directors are active participants at conferences and make numerous presentations. They have developed excellent relationships with trustees and staff. Their RFPs are expertly written and seem to meet most of the hurdles. However, the principals do not really commit the resources to translate the presentations to reality. The articulated "disciplines and rigorous analysis" is, in fact, more form than substance. They have not kept up with the technology in the investment management industry. Although performance has achieved 100 bp over the index in the past five years, your consulting firm's analysts do not believe that Firm C will add significant value over the long term.

You would present Firm B to your client, right? Yet, the principals at Firm B speak guttural English. Their presentations are hard to follow and they would just as soon not be bothered with client service. They are unkempt and are generally irreverent to everyone. Finally, and most importantly, they do not convey confidence that they know how to manage a business.

Now, who are you going to present? I suspect that you will present Firm A, thereby accepting an 80% probability rather than 95% probability of your client meeting the return objective. If things don't work out, well, gosh, who could blame you?

Firm B just doesn't have the total package. The idea of "serving the customer" is not in the blood of Firm B. No matter how good their product and performance, they will lose at the game of institutional investment management. And, if they lose at the business game, the undistracted implementation of the investment strategy will be more difficult.

Firm C, although it offers excellent marketers, presenters, and schmoozers, just doesn't have the horses to meet the client's objectives.

The marketing efforts will be so much easier if those characteristics that are communicated represent, in fact, the characteristics of the firm. Those characteristics can become a reality only with conscientious and diligent business planning.

THE RELATIONSHIP BETWEEN THE BUSINESS PLAN AND THE MARKETING PLAN

As outlined in the last chapter, meeting clients' requirements means running an efficient business—all aspects of that business. In effect, I believe marketing can be viewed as one of three tautological elements necessary to run a successful money management firm.

- Effective Marketing Requires:
  Effective Business Planning and Effective Investment Performance

- Effective Business Planning Requires:
  Effective Marketing and Effective Investment Performance

- Effective Investment Performance Requires:
  Effective Marketing and Effective Business Planning

The first two relationships may be obvious to the reader. Knowing who the firm is, knowing where it is going, and having achieved strong investment results provide a better story line when selling the product than a tentative firm with poor performance.

Similarly, good business planning is easier when the firm has a stable revenue base from existing clients. Of course, the likelihood of being fired diminishes with good performance. With a good marketing plan, the prospects of revenue growth are greater, and so is the ability to plan for the future.

The last relationship may seem less obvious. It shouldn't, if viewed broadly. Follow this argument:

1. The difference in long-term track records between good performing managers and poor performing managers in almost any discipline may be measured in tens of basis points.

2. Those basis points are achieved through hard work and efficient deployment of resources (costs include limited time, fundamental research, quantitative research, company visits, comfortable working space, compliance, hiring and training of staff, trading activity, etc.).

3. Business planning is simply the process of resource management. Marketing can be viewed as the process of resource maintenance and resource enhancement.

4. Without sufficient resources, investment performance *will* deteriorate. QED.

Real-world illustrations abound to prove this point.

I am reminded of an international manager employed by my organization several years ago. The founding principal ("Thomas Sully") had achieved outstanding success while on the professional staff at a blue-chip global firm. He struck out on his own with supporting clients (including several Fortune 500 companies and large public plans) and positive endorsements by major consulting firms. Joining Thomas Sully Associates were a limited number of professionals with whom he had previously worked. All professional staff were offered meaningful equity participation.

For the first year or two, the firm's performance was pretty good. However, Tom Sully had always had back-office support and the security of resources from a large organization, but he was now faced with the new task of resource planning. As a workaholic, Tom tried to do too much himself— portfolio management, administration, and marketing. As a client and a friend, it became quite obvious to me that he was spreading himself much too thin.

Within two years of start-up, one of his colleagues left Thomas Sully Associates to return to a very large money manager. This was a significant event, not only because of the possible impact on short-term performance, but as a reflection of the health of the firm's working environment. Usually, investment professionals dream of being principals in a start-up operation and to abandon that dream likely means that something is running amok.

Soon, not surprisingly, investment performance began to deteriorate.

One could say that the markets moved against Thomas Sully Associates, and his style would come back into favor. This, of course, was the argument that Tom himself made. Although impossible to prove definitively, I believe that the major reason for the poor performance can be traced to poor business planning and to the draining of resources spent trying to grow the business.

Thomas Sully Associates lost a couple of key clients, lost the support of the consulting firms, and eventually folded up its tent.

The point is clear: Adherence to sound business planning principles, effective marketing, and good investment decisions must be practiced at all times. I believe that if the firm manages the components of the business well and keeps in mind their interrelationships, that firm increases its probability of success.

EVALUATION OF ALTERNATIVE MARKETING ACTIVITIES

The marketing plan may call for many different strategies, all of which cost money. If the perceived and cumulative impact of individual marketing strategies is positive, the manager should do everything short of bankruptcy and compromising the investment process to ensure that enough resources are available to this critical activity. However, as Tom Sully learned, advisors must also avoid spending just to spend.

Many kinds of marketing activity can be identified. I have classified them into seven groups.

1. Calling/Mailing of background and performance information to potential clients.

   Every money manager should spend a week on the other side of the table. The number of unsolicited phone calls and mailings received by plan sponsor staff (and some board members) is absolutely astounding. There are periods where my wastebasket fills up to the top with unread, unwanted information from money managers. Much of it was sent via Federal Express. Why, oh why, do money managers do this to me and every other plan sponsor? The cost of these mailings to advisors must be huge.

How many ways can I say it: **Mass mailings do not work and are a waste of money!!!**

As far as phone calls are concerned, most plan sponsors who are actively developing new investment programs and mounds of administrative activities do not have time to speak with callers. Those that do have the time and agree to meet probably are not doing anything innovative anyway.

Obviously, if a manager is visiting an area and wants to make contact with a known plan sponsor, a phone call to arrange a meeting is appropriate. It would be best if the phone call and visit were accompanied by:

  a. Information that the plan sponsor is doing something similar to what the advisor is offering;

  b. Recent, positive press or a published article about some product or research innovation; or

  c. Recent contact with the plan sponsor at a conference, seminar, or other function.

2. Initial and follow-up presentations to potential clients.

Generating new contacts among targeted organizations is an activity that every manager participates in to some degree. Getting in front of clients is an important objective. Even if no search is currently being undertaken, establishing name and product recognition is extremely worthwhile.

The opportunity to meet potential clients is more likely if the manager provides something in return. Rarely is learning about firm and the product itself all that motivating. Therefore, initiating meetings should be combined with developing a high profile for the firm and its principals through the activities that are outlined below (points 3 through 7).

Once the opportunity to meet is provided, *don't blow it*. Address the nine hurdles succinctly and in turn. A formally prepared presentation delivered informally is the key. Those firms that can address the hurdles in a professional, personable manner—and can react to individual client needs and culture—will get a leg up when formal searches are being conducted.

Presentations can take place in one of three places: the client's office, the advisor's office, or informally over lunch or dinner. Of course, the best place to show a firm's strengths is in its own office. Few advisors know how to take advantage of this opportunity: showing a bunch of messy desks and Bloombergs does not really convey much of anything to the sponsor. Visits to work areas and introductions to professional staff should be woven naturally into the presentation.

My view is that, for the serious plan sponsor staff, paying for lunch, dinner, and other entertainment is a waste of time and money. The same holds for most committee/board members; however, sometimes this is the only way to gain access and may be necessary. In today's world of careful oversight and liability avoidance, the success of entertainment as a strategy to win business is marginal.

3. Initial and follow-up presentations to consultants.

My own, unsubstantiated view is that it is impossible to spend too much time with the major consultants. It is always best to meet at the advisor offices, but usually that takes place only after the client or consultant has a high level of interest.

Most consultants will meet with most money management firms that have any credibility at all. Frustration may arise, of course, in attempting to get the attention of the senior consultants. If initial meetings can be arranged only with junior consultants, do not get angry. Advisors should meet and give them their best effort. Junior consultants often do have influence with more senior people and may become senior one day themselves. Similar overviews to plan sponsors should be presented, but preparations should be made to go into much more detail if desired.

Advisors should get into the consultants' heads and ask why they should be presented to their clients. When meeting with consultants, competitive strengths and differentiating features should be reviewed early on in the presentation.

4. Co-sponsoring external industry conferences.

Many opportunities exist to co-sponsor seminars coordinated by professional groups (e.g., Institutional Investor, Investment Management Institute, International Investment Research, Pensions & Investment). It is difficult for me to assess the cost-effectiveness of these seminars. Everything else being equal, it never hurts to use these vehicles to get the name out.

I do not make a habit of attending. The material is generally very introductory and the quality is mixed. Those conferences held in resorts tend to be even more so. Finally, the ratio of managers to sponsors is high, and those sponsors that attend are often lower-level or new board/committee members who may have little real influence.

At the risk of offending a great many people who make livings off these conferences, my gut tells me that the few extra contacts made are not worth the cost for most of these conferences. Anybody seriously interested in the conference topics can access the information much more efficiently and directly.

5. Co-sponsoring external educational seminars.

I distinguish educational seminars from industry conferences by the extensiveness of the agenda. Seminars sponsored by Association for Investment Management Research (AIMR), Pension Real Estate Association (PREA), Institute for Fiduciary Education (IFE), Elkind Economics, and some consulting organizations are representative of this group. The attendees usually include a more serious-minded group of portfolio managers and plan sponsors for a simple reason: marketing directors are less numerous. Hence, the seminars are more enjoyable and worthwhile for plan sponsors.

The advantage of this activity for the advisor is clear: there is increased opportunity for more meaningful dialog and relationship building with the target audience. This is particularly true for the more exclusive seminars, which offer firm principals a forum to show off their smarts and investment management skills.

The flip side is that the cost of some of these (e.g., IFE, Elkind Economics) can be astronomical. Is the cost worth it? I do not know. I do know that many of the firms sponsoring these seminars have won valuable accounts. Perhaps they would have won them anyway.

Cost aside, there is no question in my mind that the educational seminars are far more valuable public relations tools than mass mailings and boondoggle conferences.

6. Sponsoring in-house client educational seminars.

Some of the large managers provide periodic seminars for their clients and "invited guests" (i.e., potential clients). It does not hurt to reinforce goodwill with existing clients. I seriously doubt, however, that client-sponsored conferences will influence hiring/retaining decisions. Actually, I can think of three reasons why they may be a negative.

First, some clients look at these as a frittering away of money: "How can we justify wasting the plan's money on food, wine, and tee-times?"

Second, if the manager has problems, it provides an opportunity for clients to get together and grouse. Little problems, if shared with others, may now be perceived by those clients as significant.

Third, turning down an invitation from a business supplier is uncomfortable. I do not enjoy telling the marketing/client service director that I cannot come when I know he or she is under pressure to build attendance.

The fact is that plan sponsors do not need money managers to provide a forum to meet industry luminaries or to get together with brethren to schmooze. There are plenty of other opportunities to pursue these goals.

7. Active research and journal publications.

One of the best ways to develop name recognition is overlooked by managers. Advisors achieve prominence by adding something to the industry's state of the art. When sponsors decide to allocate their time, they do so when they get something back in return. Maybe that is a free meal. Often, it is the opportunity to meet people who are intelligent and have used that intelligence. Also, a little fame doesn't hurt.

People who demonstrate creativity and innovation in a broader forum will be perceived by many to be creative and innovative at their investment management firm.

Each one of these activities requires resources that cost money, including: dedicated marketing professionals, investment professional time, systems and clerical support to create and maintain an information database, postage and telephone usage, travel, systems/staff support for producing marketing material and RFP responses, and many other costs.

Before expenditures are allocated, each possible marketing activity should affirmatively answer one or both of the following questions:

1. Does the expenditure improve the *ability* to communicate to the important decision makers the message necessary to overcome the hurdles articulated in Chapter 3?

2. Does the expenditure improve the *opportunity* to communicate to the important decision makers the message necessary to overcome the hurdles articulated in Chapter 3?

Activities then should be ranked according to their anticipated marginal contribution to revenue enhancement, and expenditure decisions should be made accordingly. Ideally, a tracking system should be established that measures how contact was made and with whom, what meetings were held and with whom, what searches were participated in and what accounts won. Over long periods of time, patterns of success and failure may emerge.

PREPARING FOR THE PRESENTATION AND SOCIAL ETIQUETTE

The agency relationship inevitably creates discomfort for plan sponsor purchasers of money management services. This discomfort arises from insecurity from lack of technical experience or, more likely as plan sponsor staffs become more sophisticated, general skepticism toward the added value that managers claim. Sometimes plan sponsors experience both insecurity and skepticism. The marketing plan must strive to overcome these feelings.

To return to my analogy in Chapter 1, the Drake Beam trick to effective marketing was: (1) to be clear as to one's own competitive advantages; (2) to identify those organizations who may find one's competitive advantages desirable; (3) to ascertain the profile of the key players and the decision-making processes of those organizations; and (4) to establish timely communications with those key players and organizations. In short, we were advised to get to know and to understand the marketplace *before* trying to sell ourselves. Reference was made in Chapters 1 and 2 to the fact that much of the marketing effort should be made before personal contact is established.

One cannot minimize the importance of preparation. Certainly, it takes time, effort, and money to prepare properly before important meetings. Yet, managers will spend significant resources flying around the country at a moment's notice, hours in airports and taxis, weeks and months preparing presentation reports—but only a few minutes researching the historical context of the targeted pension plan and the perspectives of the decision makers.

Once advisors are able to arrange interviews with plan sponsors, the strategy is usually to attempt to explain their particular firms' special, competitive advantages. Although rarely implemented effectively, this strategy of distinguishing uniqueness from the thousands of other advisors is the right one.

Yet, often these same advisors strangely presume that the character of each individual plan sponsor audience is no different from that of their industry brethren. Not only is the presumption inaccurate, but this attitude, when signalled, will undermine much of what they are trying to communicate.

When I felt as though advisors were lumping me with "other corporate plans" or "other retirement systems" or "other plan sponsor professionals," I would play a little game. Through innuendo, I would imply how they and other managers did this or that. Inevitably, the response elicited would be, "Yes, that may be true of most advisors, but we are different." Depending on my mood, I would retort, "If you think you are so special, why don't you offer me the same courtesy and respect associated with being a unique, multidimensional professional?"

Historically, the practice of investment management was considered an arcane specialty. To some degree, unlike practitioners in law and medicine, "iconoclasts" and "oddballs" might have been accepted to some degree (maybe even preferred) because it takes creative genius to make money. However, I think that the tolerance for deviant behavior is less than it used to be.

With the greater level of sophistication among senior executives, the technical mystery of investment management has lessened and the demands for accountability have increased. Taking "brilliance" on faith does not work any more among the educated. It is no longer enough for advisors to come before committees once per year, in bowties, spouting euphemisms and platitudes for thirty minutes. One fellow I remember would mix a very erudite discussion on economic theory, having very little basis in fact, with simple platitudes. I am not sure that his firm's business prospects are as strong as they once were unless his approach has modified.

With the formalization of presentation has come a formalization of social behavior expectations. Proper professional etiquette must be practiced. I have identified sixteen etiquette rules.

1. Do not make enemies by going behind somebody's back. There is nothing wrong with establishing good relations with more than one person at any targeted organization, but be up front about it.

   During the process of studying structural alternatives of his company's guaranteed investment contract (GIC) portfolio, a colleague of mine talked with several GIC advisors. One of these got a bright idea of establishing a "professional" relationship with one of his board members. One afternoon a sales meeting was arranged with the board member, the CFO, the treasurer, my friend, and the advisor to discuss GICs. Needless to say, the entire corporate staff was grossly offended and would never, ever pursue business with this firm.

Another manager consistently comes to Olympia to meet with the members of my current employer, The Washington State Investment Board. Occasionally, if free time is available between these meetings, the manager will call me—The Chief Investment Officer. Although I will continue to evaluate firms objectively, this fellow's treatment of me as second fiddle does not sit well. Since I have some say about bringing the best firms to my board for interviews, this manager is acting foolishly. To their credit, even some of the board members have made unsolicited comments about this manager spending too much time schmoozing. All this suggests that all his efforts are actually having the opposite effect from what is intended.

All this is not to say that establishing good relations with board or committee members is not a good idea. However, money managers should be certain to let staff and the consultants know the marketing plan. In most instances, they will not have a problem.

2. Be on time to meetings. The money manager has no control over plane delays and snowstorms. However, the manager can avoid scheduling too many meetings that are likely to run long, and he should have maps to each destination. Calling from the car phone in traffic or from the tollway in the next town after making a wrong turn does not cut it. Being late conveys the message that the plan sponsor's time is not important to the money manager. Perhaps more importantly, sloppy scheduling implies sloppy business planning.

3. Arrive at meetings looking refreshed and neat. Disheveled hair and disheveled dress implies lack of control and lack of professionalism. It is better to stop at the rest room to clean up and be two minutes late than to appear unkempt.

4. Do not bring armies of people to meetings. Two people is the optimal number, three at the most. While one individual is interacting, the other one or two can observe body language and insert comments at appropriate times to smooth out the rough spots during conversations.

With greater numbers of principals, defensiveness increases significantly. "Off-the-record" discourses and trust are precluded when many unknown individuals are present. Informality and rapport simply cannot be established in a large social setting.

Two or three key principals should be able to handle any reasonable questions that come up. If the plan sponsor perceives that the manager feels that more are necessary, it implies that those principals possess little control over the business and the investment process.

5. The less integral the marketer is to the management of the business and the investment strategy of the firm, the less he should converse. It is fine to have a marketer present whose function it is to orchestrate the business development process but, once contact is made, he should shut up. Generally speaking, no one cares what he has to say.

If marketing is only one hat that the individual wears, he should participate in presentations. However, the marketer must be able to hold his own in the discussion.

6. Avoid ostentatious behavior. If taking a stretch limousine to a prospect's office is necessary, managers would be wise not to have it hang around waiting. In the age of corporate cutbacks and controls on government spending, this communicates profligacy. In the same vein, managers who show up at client meetings in obviously expensive, designer suits are likely to be viewed as supercilious. Discussions about recent vacations in Tuscany are no-nos.

Once I received a photograph of a money manager's Christmas party. Some of the women at the firm, pictured sprawled out in the front row, were scantily dressed and quite provocative. By the time the card made it to my in-box, it had been handled by most of the people in my office. Needless to say, it was several months before the snickering stopped as I walked by my colleagues' desks.

"Hey, Halpern, how come you never invite us on your overnight trips to visit managers? You sure seemed happy the last time you got back." What does that convey about the manager?

7. Be confident and assertive, but not aggressive. Recently, one manager actually became angry when I continued to bombard him with questions on the firm's philosophy and strategy. It was quite obvious

to him that I lacked faith in something that was so obvious to him and anyone else with half a brain. His show of anger at "my ignorance, density, and pigheadedness" will be unlikely to win him any business.

This manager believed in his program, which is good, but was not able to present his case convincingly to me. The process and philosophy of a management firm must be at the plan sponsor's disposal, not foisted on him. The manager can cajole but not force the plan sponsor to desire the firm's wares.

8. Convey understanding, but avoid overfamiliarity.

A theme of this book is to understand your audience: their trials and tribulations. Only by appreciating the war and battles that the sponsor wages in his or her career can the manager convincingly argue for the merits of the firm's weapons.

Be clear, however, that understanding and familiarity are two quite distinct concepts. Most people have a close-knit group of friends and these people do not have agendas. If your agenda is to be nice only to gain business, you are likely not my friend. Friendliness and feigned friendship are rarely confused by the recipient. One is appreciated; the other is not.

Along these lines, I have a very handy system with my secretary. Since people who know me know that I prefer to be called Philip, callers who are my "intimate friends" asking for "Phil" always are courteously asked to make contact by mail only.

9. Do not try to impress by being "well-connected and industry-wise." The fact is that it takes a very short time before most people in the industry know most other people in the industry. A large network in and of itself is not impressive. Also, assume that most plan sponsors can discriminate between the "hype of scuttlebutt" and significant trends.

Along these same lines, nothing offends plan sponsors more quickly than an expression of false empathy with their job demands after only the most cursory, introductory pleasantries. Whether people are found in the corporate suite or a cocktail party, they do not communicate in the same way, entertain the same level of interest, nor possess the same hot buttons. Presuming that you know your audience *before* you do your homework is a big mistake.

10. Be consistent in your message. One anecdote illustrates the importance of consistency.

While managing the investment portfolio at J.C. Penney, I had met with a Japanese firm who had developed a very attractive multifactor model. Although I had not had the opportunity to recommended them to my Investment Committee before moving to my current employer, I was intrigued by their product. This firm had the qualities that I personally found attractive: a quantitative approach that produced consistent, positive returns.

Once at The Washington State Investment Board, I agreed to meet with them in order to renew our relationship. To my surprise, the portfolio manager and lead marketing executive were not the people I had met nor did they discuss the product in which I had an interest. The presentation that they prepared described a fundamental, stock-picking process. After about ten minutes of introductory pleasantries, I asked them what was going on. I was told that public plan prospects were not shown the more technically complex product, but the one presented that day.

Given my own quantitative orientation and previous relationship with the firm, what were they thinking? They made two unacceptable mistakes. First, they completely evaporated the existing goodwill that they had built up with me because they were insensitive to my interests. Second, the firm implied that public plan professionals were too stupid to understand sophisticated investment techniques.

You can be sure that it will a cold day in Hades before this firm is recommended by me to my board.

11. Do not overly rely on the "halo effect." A positive signal is emitted when other smart people have decided to employ a certain strategy or hire a certain firm. However, most sponsors have their own ideas. Just because someone else does it does not mean you should do it.

After all, an awful lot of smart people bought downtown office buildings in the late 1980s.

12. Communicate among yourselves before the presentation. On many occasions, principals from the same firm would interrupt and contradict each other at a presentation. The plan sponsor really does not care who is "right" or "wrong," since such a display precludes any hope of that firm receiving money to manage.

I had one fascinating series of interchanges with two prestigious money management subsidiaries of large parent financial institutions who were merging their investment operations into a new joint venture.

Prior to the merger, I had several meetings with Manager A and expressed substantial interest in pursuing discussions about a quantitatively based, foreign equity strategy. When Manager B called I agreed to meet, and it quickly became apparent that Manager B was selling an almost identical process and performance record. When I inquired what was going on, Manager B stated that it would be a couple of months before the two would formally merge and they remained competitors until that time. I was informed that Manager B would be willing to cut the price significantly in order to get my business (i.e., the firm wanted their cut before any revenue-sharing plan was instituted). When I confronted Manager A with my discovery, they in turn offered to negotiate price.

For several weeks, I enjoyed the competition between Manager A and Manager B. I would receive a call every couple of days from one or the other offering sweeter and sweeter deals. Finally, the two chairmen got together and called me to suggest that they would like to revise their proposals to reflect a "joint" effort. As it so happens, I was about to leave my employer and the joint proposal ended up going nowhere.

13. It should be obvious that talking about politics and controversial issues is done at your own peril. As hard as it may be for money managers to believe, not everyone is a Republican and thinks poorly of Hillary Clinton. Once a manager spent 20 minutes lambasting

Clinton and the healthcare proposals without having any idea of my beliefs. As a matter of record, Washington state has a Democratic governor and passed a statewide, comprehensive healthcare plan in 1994.

In the public sector, this caution is particularly apt. An example occurred at a recent meeting of The Washington State Investment Board. The chairman of the board of a major tobacco company spoke to the Investment Board, its largest shareholder through a general partnership vehicle, about business prospects at his company. By extolling growth potential in expanding demographic groups and minimizing relative health hazards, the chairman inadvertently undercut the political agenda of some of the board members to reduce tobacco smoking in the state. In spite of the excellent returns earned by the general partner, these kinds of insensitivities will complicate the GP's future capital-raising efforts.

14. Do not arrange to receive phone calls or faxes while on marketing calls. I cannot tell you how many times I have been annoyed at having to deliver a fax to a money manager. Unless you are a friend, do not interrupt my business with your business. If a plan sponsor is willing to meet with a money manager, that money manager should have the courtesy not to be thinking of other things.

15. Avoid using sports analogies unless you know the client. Not everyone watches sports or understands that blitzes do not refer to a special kind of pastry. Some people prefer reading Naguib Mafouz to watching Monday night football. Even if one is a sports fan, these analogies too often come across as vapid cliches.

16. Finally, be prepared to relinquish control of the floor to the client at any time. There is a fine line between controlling the flow of information and allowing the client to go in the direction that he or she desires. Quite honestly, few individuals are effective at this balance.

Managers should realize that the same level of interest in what is being discussed is rarely present for most plan sponsors. Thus, it is crucial that money managers hit the important points quickly and with enthusiasm, and ignore the litany of details. Focus on the three or four themes that you would like your audience to remember. Regardless of the rapport that may develop, the audience is unlikely to remember much from the meeting one week later.

I will add one more item to the list: when presenting at educational conferences, do not go into a sales pitch for the firm! Nothing in the world is tackier to clients or potential clients than going to a public forum to gain insights from experts and then being blatantly sold to.

Recently my staff prepared a client symposium for my Board and invited all 16 domestic and international equity managers. The rules of the game required that managers were to educate the board, not attempt to sell their wares. (Of course, in reality, the best selling is done when sharing knowledge and insight, not when "selling.") One of the advisors went into a diatribe on his firm's product lasting for 40 minutes—nearly twice the allocated time slot. This advisor's brazen attitude offended not only the staff and the other managers who had prepared general capital market information, but also the Board members.

I observed another manager performing the same stunt at an overseas seminar sponsored by IFE. Several chief investor officers commented that the guilty manager would go to the bottom of their list when considering international equity candidates. What is ironic is that this manager spent many thousands of dollars to gain access to this group of institutional investors only to damage severely his cause.

Each item on this list of social etiquette rules really amounts to the same thing: treat the plan sponsor with respect and do not attempt to "bowl over" the client. Although seemingly difficult for many managers to stomach, this respect must be real, not feigned. Businessmen and government leaders may or may not be investment professionals, but most who have achieved success can smell insincerity miles away. If respect is practiced consciously long enough at client meetings, the money manager may actually internalize this respect.

This simple truth might seem trivial but, in reality, is understood by few: people are most comfortable doing business with others who share similar values and beliefs. Sensitivity by money managers should be heightened especially when interacting with decision makers from a different organizational culture and/or socioeconomic background. Principals of money management firms who communicate attitudes offensive to their target audience are dead meat.

To paraphrase another in a more noble context than this, "It is not what the plan sponsor can do for the money manager, but what the money manager can do for the plan sponsor."

CONCLUDING THOUGHTS

Marketing to existing clients and prospects should not be considered a distraction from the real business of managing money. In this chapter, several key elements for marketing success have been reviewed.

1. The importance of building an organization that not only is likely to produce performance results but is likely to meet the characteristics of an advisory firm desired by the target audience.

2. The importance of meeting characteristics desired by the client by integrating the business plan and the marketing plan with the investment program.

3. The importance of evaluating the benefits of various marketing strategies with respect to costs.

4. The importance of preparing for presentations and of practicing proper etiquette.

The outstanding marketing organization is characterized by both formal and informal elements. The formal elements include the institutionalization of a planning process. The informal elements include the ability to read the nuances of people and new situations and to adjust quickly to individual opportunities. These two elements are not unlike those necessary to implement an outstanding portfolio management program. And the marketing efforts should be undertaken with as much zeal and forethought as the investment manager employs in building a portfolio of companies.

Chapter 6

REQUEST FOR PROPOSALS AND THE SEARCH

M ost consultants and public plans, and some private plans, issue questionnaires to advisors in order to garner information used in formal manager searches. Request for Proposals (RFPs) range in length from a few pages to several hundred depending on the organization or assignment. The steps of the process usually proceed in the following manner:

Step 1: Staff/consultant recommendation to invest using a new strategy/advisor

Step 2: Board/committee approval of the recommendation

Step 3: Issuance of request for proposals

Step 4: Staff/consultant evaluation of strongest candidates

Step 5: Board interviews of finalists and selection of advisor

The underlying characteristic of a formal RFP decision-making process is the objective evaluation and selection in steps 4 and 5. I cannot honestly say that all RFPs, everywhere, all the time, are objective. I do believe, however, that most searches are fair.

Advisors who most effectively address the hurdles articulated in Chapter 3 have the best chance of winning the competition. Business development strategies that rely more on informal schmoozing with consultants, investment staff, and board/committee members do not excuse advisors from having to overcome these same hurdles.

The same RFP questions, or close variations, discussed in this chapter will be asked in all advisor searches, whether the searches are conducted formally or informally, whether advisors are dealing in public market securities or are general partners investing in venture capital companies.

The point is this: **Advisors who develop the same rigor of response that can marshal them successfully through the formal RFP game can use those same attributes to win business through other manager selection processes.** The trick is to be consistent and thorough when communicating in all marketing situations.

Both the form and content of the information provided is crucial to managers' ultimate success rate in being hired. Although completing the RFP questionnaire is an arduous project, the effort is important. A halfhearted effort simply will not work.

THE FIRM'S IDENTITY AND THE APPROPRIATE RFP RESPONSE

Responses to RFPs must reflect the identity of the firm and the firm's stage in its own business life cycle. Appropriate and consistent responses are particularly important in meeting the soft hurdles.

Money management firms can be categorized into one of three general groups. First are the emerging firms with few institutional clients who are in the start-up phase of business development. These firms obviously have the hardest task in filling out the RFP and must spend the most time on this section. Even for plans that seek out emerging managers, the credibility obstacle will be a serious one to overcome. This is because the board/committee member could be criticized for hiring a particular emerging manager should performance be poor. For the emerging manager to be hired, it must overcome this negative in the mind of the board/committee member.

This first group of managers could be well served by bringing in other credible groups as advisors or owners. This would substantiate that, even though new to the industry, the firm had been checked out thoroughly by another credible source. One strategy might be to provide letters of reference from well-known individuals and organizations. The emerging managers' principals should demonstrate a personal history of stability and success. Finally, a solid history of managing the product at another institution would be a key prerequisite for success.

A second group of managers are those who have a few quality clients, but are still actively building name recognition and growth. These managers have credibility in the marketplace, but may not be known to board/committee members. In this case, the history of the firm may not provide unquestioned comfort but it can more easily demonstrate credibility than the emerging manager. Thus, from the board/committee perspective, they probably will not be criticized for hiring a manager from this group.

The third and last group of managers are those with a solid group of top-notch clients, a significant asset base, and a long track record that probably reflects consistently good performance. Obviously, this group has reached the level of success to which the previous groups aspire.

The obstacle that this group must overcome is the perception that they may be getting fat and happy. This group must respond to possible charges of increasing bureaucracy, loss of interest and control by the top principals, and an asset base too large to implement the strategies that have been successful in the past.[1]

Each of the three groups must describe where they are in their life cycle and the resulting issues that need to be resolved by those evaluating the RFP responses. A successful response to the firm's description is an absolutely necessary condition, but not sufficient for employment.

REAL-LIFE RFP RESPONSES

Questions in the RFP tend to be grouped into six general areas, which are designed implicitly to test the manager on the nine hurdles.

    A. Description of the Firm

    B. Organization

C. Product Philosophy and Investment Process

D. Performance and Performance Attributes

E. Client Service

F. Fees

The examples illustrated in this chapter are based on live RFP submissions to The Washington State Investment Board. Although the basis for the examples is publicly available information, modifications have been made and the firm names changed. The examples to be discussed have been chosen for their representativeness or effectiveness in addressing the hurdles.

Responses to questions on fees are straightforward—they are what the advisor says they are. I will hold my comments on fees until Chapter 7.

A. Description of the Firm

The first section of the RFP usually queries applicants about the firm and their qualifications. When addressing the first set of questions, the smart advisor will set the tone for the investment themes necessary to address the strategic hurdles. However, the advisor must craft the responses to target the soft hurdles: credibility, credentials, comfort from others, and responsiveness.

A1. Please give a brief history of the firm.

Example A1-1

Thomas Eakin, Inc.'s, history as a manager of tax-exempt assets parallels that of our predecessor organizations: NAH Investment Advisors, a wholly owned subsidiary of NAH established in 1984; and The American Bank Trust Department, established in 1903. Our firm's senior investment professionals launched one of the nation's first non-U.S. equity funds in 1974. Our present non-U.S. investment approach, which has been in place for 12 years, has been to evaluate all non-U.S. markets in a global context. Our ability to manage a Europe-only equity portfolio is evidenced by our investment experience across non-U.S. markets.

Thomas Eakin, Inc., evolved from NAH Investment Advisors and was registered as an SEC investment advisor in 1989. The firm was established under a transfer of ownership structure within which all aspects of the prior organizations dating from 1980—philosophy, process, and people—remain in place.

Comments:

Example A1-1 illustrates how a manager focuses on the positive. Language is carefully chosen to convey this image. By responding about its "predecessor" organization, continuity with its past, and hence credibility, is established. In addition, Thomas Eakin focuses on its pedigree through reference to its trust roots with a blue-blood institution back at the turn of the century. The fact that the manager has gone through major reorganizations and the current management team has no relation to that of yesteryear gets lost in the response.

Thomas Eakin is a pretty nifty dancer: it does not state why the firm adopted its current structure. Interestingly, the advisor plays with the chronological order of the response in order to establish credibility before mentioning the management buyout. And, of course, "transfer of ownership structure" is much nicer than buyout. In fact, only the astute reader can really understand the transfer from whom to whom.

The firm also makes reference to its creativity and innovation by launching into its roots in international investing. Of course, the manager is being somewhat selective in its use of "one of the nation's first non-U.S. equity funds." Other international investment vehicles were offered to U.S. investors, but most of these were provided by non-U.S. institutions.

A2. Please discuss the overall business objectives of your firm with respect to future growth over the next five years. Comment on any present or planned areas of growth over the near future. Be sure to include in your response both the subject product and any new products.

Example A2-1

Current plans are to limit the amount of assets under management to approximately $1 billion for this product. When firm assets reach that level, new business development will cease. We will then operate with those assets under management for 6 to 12 months to ascertain whether performance standards and management approach can be continued.

Remington & Associates has 30 accounts as of December 31, 1994, which should not be increased much as current assets are over $ 800 million. The separate account minimum was raised to $40 million in 1993 to help limit the number of new clients, although the firm plans to measure its limits based on assets rather than number of accounts it will accept.

All accounts are managed on a team basis, with an average of 8–10 accounts per investment professional. We feel our current staff is sufficient to continue providing excellent results and service to our clients, but we are prepared to add one or two professionals if necessary.

Example A2-2

Over the next few years Wyeth Company will seek additional clients among each of its major divisions—Fixed-Income, Equities, and International. Given the size and liquidity of the markets, we can increase fixed-income assets without sacrificing the integrity of our investment style. In addition, we have sufficient staff to handle the expected account growth for 1996.

We expect strong growth in both our Equity and International divisions over the next few years. Wyeth Company's Equity Division has great growth potential relative to the staff's abilities and capacities. Regarding the value equity product, we are sufficiently staffed to handle up to $2 billion in assets, at which point we would add staff if needed. We are well positioned to accept new clients in our international area as this investment area continues to spark heightened interest. Our primary concern is to maintain a proactive client service program, and we will do so by continuing to add to professional staff as we acquire additional clients.

Example A2-3

Bierstadt's primary goal is to continue to provide top-notch growth stock investment management to U.S.-based, tax-exempt, institutional funds. We at Bierstadt, Inc., strive to achieve long-term growth of our clients' capital through the management of emerging growth stock portfolios, using an approach that focuses on growth trend analysis and fundamental analysis.

We recognize that superior performance may be affected by size of assets within the emerging growth sector. Because our primary concern is the performance of client portfolios, we have placed a target of $500 million on assets under management; at such time as we reach this amount, we will evaluate the feasibility of accepting additional assets.

Example A2-4

In respect to future growth of its business, Sargent Trust focuses on two areas: asset growth in existing disciplines and growth through the introduction of new disciplines. The depth of Sargent's resources and the diversity of our disciplines have allowed us to grow as an organization without straining the capacity of a single discipline. As we continue to grow, account by account, we closely monitor the size of the assets in each discipline and will limit asset growth when necessary. For example, several of our smaller-cap strategies have been closed to new assets. For our Premier Equity Discipline, we will not exceed $500 million in assets managed against small-cap benchmarks such as the Russell 2000 Index, and will not exceed 15 accounts per portfolio manager. The mid-cap applications will be capped at $2 billion.

Sargent Trust is dedicated to reinvesting in its future. As our business grows, we continue our practice of adding investment, executive, administrative, and support personnel to complement our asset growth. Moreover, we continue to improve our systems, research capabilities, personnel, and investment approaches to meet the evolving demands of our clients and the changes in the marketplace.

Example A2-5

Cassat Investment Advisors has two goals:

1. To be a premier investment firm providing consistently superior, value-added investment products and quality client services that improve our clients' investment programs.

2. To build on our strengths of growth specialty, well-defined disciplines and systems, and excellent client service.

To assure that we achieve these goals, we have organized our firm into two teams dedicated to each objective—investment management and client/

service marketing. Our client service/marketing professionals initiate frequent communication with clients, enabling the investment team to concentrate fully and work together on managing growth portfolios in a variety of capitalization segments.

An important contributor to superior returns and service is controlling asset growth and the number of client relationships. In keeping with this objective, we stopped taking new clients in the Emerging Growth small-capitalization area when we reached $500 million; New Emerging Growth clients are added only to replace existing accounts or assets. We also reached our goal at $150 million in the Mini-Cap area.

Based on similar analyses in the Mid-Cap area, we intend to limit Mid-Cap to $4 billion at current market levels; Convertible to $500 million; Hedge to $500 million; and International Growth to $5 billion.

Our growth goals are determined by total assets—not by the number of accounts. Relationships are limited to 30 to 40 for each client service professional.

Our staffing will always be a function of client needs, market environments, growth investment opportunities, liquidity constraints, opportunities to add talented investment and client service professionals, and quality control.

Comments:

A well-thought-out business plan indicates that the firm has planned for its future and, consequently, has planned for the future of its clients. No credible firm can operate without a strategic plan.

Most institutional investors are concerned about the advisor acquiring too many assets and too many clients because of the effect on the firm's ability to carry out its mandates. Helter-skelter growth will impact negatively portfolio performance, client responsiveness, or both. Clients will view their importance to the advisory firm as diminished if that firm blatantly views its own revenue growth as the major goal, rather than as a by-product of outstanding performance.

Several themes emerge among these examples of firms articulating their business plans. First, the business plan reinforces broader goals or mission statements. I very much like these statements, provided that the business plan supports the stated objectives.

Bierstadt's first paragraph (example A2-3) is succinct and laudable in the conviction it expresses to achieve greatness. The two goals articulated by Cassat Investment Advisors (example A2-5) effectively couple their own business success with investment program objectives. Although both examples are somewhat hokey, they help to convey the image of the success dream.

The second theme is that all five advisors, to some degree, emphasize *quality*, not quantity, of relationships. Remington (example A2-1) and Cassat Investment Advisors (example A2-5) do the best jobs in providing evidence that they have been thinking about managing their business. They are specific about the size of assets and the number of accounts that their professional staff can handle.

Firms that have limited product lines versus broad product lines will need to address this question differently. Narrow product line organizations (e.g., Remington) have the advantage that they are focused, with fewer administrative distractions. However, firms such as Cassat with broader product offerings can leverage back-office and client service functions. In addition, should one or two products fail, the broadly based firm is more likely to survive.

The servicing differences can be seen in contrasting Remington and Cassat. Remington, the smaller firm, discusses the limitation of accounts per "investment professional," whereas Cassat discusses the limitation per "client service professional." Cassat's response indicates a subtle distinction: Cassat's dedicated professional client staff will isolate the portfolio managers from their clients much more so than will Remington.

Also, given Cassat's obviously larger product line, Cassat's client service professionals undoubtedly are compensated for product extension and identification of product development opportunities. The fact that they will continue to sell even when hired emerges when reading the following sentence closely:

> "Our client service/marketing professionals initiate frequent communication with clients, enabling the investment team

to concentrate fully and work together on managing growth portfolios in a variety of capitalization segments."

Cassat's response would have been stronger had they indicated how portfolio managers were going to interact with their clients.

For those institutional clients preferring to deal with portfolio managers, Remington's response is closer to the mark.

Wyeth Company (example A2-2), Bierstadt, Inc. (example A2-3), and Sargent Trust (example A2-4) get the "pulling the wool over clients eyes" awards. They all sound good, using such phrases as "a proactive client service program," "primary concern" for the performance of client portfolios, and so on. Yet, their defined business plans do not reflect their stated philosophy.

Wyeth provides a $2 billion limitation but, once it is hit, staff will be hired and the limitation goes up. Bierstadt also states a limitation of $500 million, but it is meaningless because they always have the flexibility to "evaluate the feasibility of accepting additional assets."

A3. Over the past five years, has your organization or any of its affiliates or parent, or any officer or principal, been involved in any business litigation or other legal proceedings related to your investment activities? If so, provide an explanation and indicate the current status.

Example A3-1

Sargent Trust has filed litigation in Nebraska state and federal courts against a former employee. The lawsuits seek to recover profits that the former employee made from an investment opportunity that Sargent believes was provided to the employee as compensation for causing accounts managed by Sargent to invest in certain securities. Any recovery from the lawsuit will be distributed to the Sargent accounts that purchased the securities at issue.

Example A3-2

In February 1988, O'Keefe Guarantee Associates (the "Company"), O'Keefe Guarantee Money Fund, Inc. (the "Fund"), and three directors of the Fund were named as defendants in an action brought on behalf of the shareholders of the Fund which, as amended, asserted a claim for excessive investment advisory fees under the Investment Company Act of 1940, a claim for breach of the Company's common law fiduciary duty, and a claim for violation of the shareholder proxy rules. The action sought, among other things, recovery of advisory fees in an unspecified amount charged to the Fund by the Company. **On August 1, 1991, the U.S. District Court for the Southern District of California dismissed the action. The U.S. Court of Appeals affirmed the District Court's judgment on November 14, 1991.**

Comments:

Litigation, compliance violations, or irregularities of any kind obviously are not good. However, we live in a complicated society where right and wrong are complicated issues. Anybody who does anything takes the chance of being slammed at some point. Advisors responding to questionnaires must be honest and thorough for both ethical reasons and legal reasons.

Sargent Trust (example A3-1) should have been more complete in its response regarding the amount in question and in which accounts. They also would be wise to address how the current compliance procedures have been modified to prevent the obvious conflict from occurring again. This half-answer could be enough for the reader to not want to deal with the uncertainty and to remove the manager from consideration.

O'Keefe Guarantee Associates were succinct in their response. Fortunately, the case was dismissed. They would be better off, however, by stating that the court decision substantiates O'Keefe's good name in carrying out their fiduciary responsibility. In addition, to the extent possible, O'Keefe should state the willingness to discuss specific details with clients or potential clients.

A4. Please describe any potential conflicts of interest your firm may have in the management of this account. Include any activities of affiliated or parent organizations, brokerage activities, investment banking activities, or any existing or prior arrangements or relationships with any current WSIB board member. Include any other pertinent activities, actions, or relationships not specifically outlined in this question.

Example A4-1

While potential conflicts of interest are inherent in the investment management arena, we make every effort to insure that actual conflicts of
interest do not develop. O'Keefe Guarantee does not have an ownership
interest in any of the brokers we currently utilize. O'Keefe Guarantee
Investment Services, our wholly owned subsidiary, is a registered broker/
dealer organized in 1990 to act as principal underwriter and distributor
for the O'Keefe Guarantee Funds. While expanding its activities in 1994
to include a discount brokerage service, it does not conduct securities
transactions for our investment counsel clients or the O'Keefe Guarantee
Funds.

Comments:

Conflicts of interest, both real and perceived, must be avoided at all cost.
Investment advisors wishing to vertically integrate must do so cautiously
and maintain independent activities. O'Keefe's broker/dealer activities
should be acceptable to most clients because their structure seems to
prevent self-dealing.

A5. Please give details on the number, name, and asset value of terminated,
    U.S.-tax-exempt, institutional client relationships in the past three
    years with reasons for the termination for the subject product.

Example A5-1

In 1991, Remington & Associates lost management of the Pierre Bonard
Family Foundation, which was $30 million. The termination was due to the
foundation's change in consultant, and therefore change in objective and
managers. This was the only account lost by Remington & Associates in
the last three years.

Example A5-2

There have been no client terminations for the subject product since
Wyeth Company's inception in 1988.

Comments:

Terminations can happen for nonperformance reasons: change in objectives like Remington's previous client, acquisition of the client corporation

and merging of plans, liquidation of assets, etc. All these reasons are legitimate and should not reflect poorly on the manager.

I have never read an RFP that accurately stated that a client was lost because of poor performance or poor client servicing. The advisor must assume that clients will check references and find out about terminations. Should the advisor neglect to mention terminations or be less than honest, he should assume that the potential client and/or consultant will uncover the truth. I have eliminated an otherwise well-qualified manager because I knew for a fact that he was bamboozling me.

A firm that does anything creative and new will risk client dissatisfaction. Fessing up to past problems and discussing lessons learned, if communicated well, can actually enhance manager credibility.

B. Organization

Like the section describing the firm, questions about the organization also focus primarily on the soft hurdles. However, the structure of the organization is under the principals' control and should reflect *directly* the investment philosophy, strategy, and process of the strategic hurdles. The principals cannot help that the firm is young or immediately control how many institutions are clients; but they can control the decision-making process and the number of investment professionals on staff.

The money manager has more ability to posture these RFP responses and, hence, influence the perceptions of the reader.

Personnel Changes

B1. Have any senior personnel left or joined the firm in the past three years? If so, please indicate when and why. In which products were they involved?

Example B1-1

Thomas Eakin, Inc., manages assets collectively on a team basis, which minimizes any potential disruption turnover could have on our investment process. **Continuity of management, therefore, is always maintained**. Management of our non-U.S. equity portfolios utilizes the efforts of all professionals within and across each asset class.

In 1992, Ben Johnson, formerly a Partner and Director of our London Office (13 years with the firm), left to pursue other career opportunities. He was replaced by James Boswell, Partner, who had previously worked closely with Mr. Johnson in our London office. This was not of major significance to the management of our non-U.S. equity portfolios since Mr. Johnson's primary area of responsibility was non-dollar bonds.

Example B1-2

During 1991 a Managing Director in the convertible area resigned as Wyeth Company made a strategic decision to de-emphasize this asset class. He had been with the firm since 1976. The Equity Division presently handles convertible relationships.

The Chairman and Chief Executive Officer left to start her own investment-related firm.

Comments:

Thomas Eakin makes it clear that continuity of management and team approach is embedded in portfolio management. The firm recognizes that turnover can be a problem right upfront and, thus, has structured the management of the firm to minimize its negative impact. This approach is very effective and instills firm control and credible management.

When turnover occurred in the case of Mr. Johnson, a qualified individual was in place to take over. The reader is left assuming that if another individual should leave, the firm has backup procedures in place. Well done, Thomas Eakin, Inc.

In contrast, the events at Wyeth and their response leave one wondering. Why were convertible bonds de-emphasized and was the decision taken before or after this individual left? And why would the Chairman leave and when did it happen? If she left to start a new firm, does this reflect that a change in strategy has taken place at Wyeth? What procedures were in place to ensure continuity?

B2. What specific incentives are employed to ensure key professionals do not leave the firm, either as a group or individually?

Example B2-1

Thomas Eakin, Inc., uses several quantitative and qualitative incentives to ensure the retention of our key senior investment professionals. Since our senior investment professionals represent the underlying assets of our firm, they have executed "noncompete" agreements. Additionally, senior investment professionals have meaningful ownership interests in the firm. We feel employee ownership combined with our participative management structure provides a strong foundation for stability and career growth. We believe that our people know that they can fulfill their own personal needs and goals within our meritocracy-driven environment.

Comments:

Thomas Eakin's response ties right into the discussion of turnover in response example B1-1. People tend not to leave because of the carrot and the stick. Thomas Eakin pays well, provides equity interest, and promotes a nice working environment. On the other hand, the noncompete clauses act as an effective disincentive to leave.

B3. Please describe your firm's backup procedures in the event the key investment professional assigned to this account should leave the firm.

Example B3-1

As previously stated, the management of Thomas Eakin's non-U.S. equity utilizes the efforts of all professionals within and across each asset class. Our firm's team composition minimizes any potential disruption of our investment process or erosive effect turnover could have on performance. Within the Account Management group, responsibilities are orchestrated by the Account Manager and shared by supporting personnel.

Example B3-2

All accounts at Remington & Associates are team managed. If one of the firm's investment professionals should leave, no disruption is anticipated in any client account. Also, although each professional is "assigned" a sector, each of them invests in all sectors. Therefore, each account is covered around the shop, and would be if one left.

Example B3-3

Wyeth Company utilizes a *team approach* to investment management. No single portfolio manager is solely responsible for any particular account. Investment decisions are made across all portfolios with similar guidelines. All portfolio managers are backed up by the investment team.

Example B3-4

Because portfolios at Bierstadt are managed on a team basis, there is no single key professional assigned to accounts.

Comments:

The theme that these advisors use to address backup procedures is clear: teamwork, teamwork, teamwork.

Thomas Eakin again nicely articulates this concept. The firm emphasizes teamwork, but also introduces the "Account Manager" as the pivot person and the person in charge of managing the account. I might also note that the Account Manager is described in a less "salesy" way than Cassat's client/service individual in example A2-5.

Remington's team approach focuses on discrete responsibility (i.e., sectors). Their response does leave one wondering how other professionals get to be knowledgeable on sectors that are not their responsibility. The same problem at Thomas Eakin arises across assets, but their response effectively glosses over the issue.

Wyeth Company's response would be more credible if it were not for example B1-2. The question arises about how intimately involved were the equity mangers in the convertible bond process before the Managing Director left? It sounds as though the Equity Division only became involved in convertible bonds *after* he left.

Finally, Bierstadt's response is a little too terse. Teamwork is terrific, but most institutions want to feel that some individual will act as a personal advocate. The tone of Bierstadt almost seems too cavalier.

The emphasis on teamwork must be tempered with control and leadership. Somebody must have the final word.

B4. Please describe your internal training procedures for portfolio managers, traders, and research analysts.

Example B4-1

Remington & Associates does not have formal training procedures. Three of the five investment pros have been with the firm since its inception. Of the other two, one is a seasoned investment pro who joined with the same basic philosophy as Remington, and the other learned by working closely on a daily basis with the entire investment team.

The firm has a team approach in its investment management and the investment pros, both young and seasoned, interact constantly, applying different perspectives on their approach. This applies to portfolio management, trading, and research analysis.

Example B4-2

Wyeth Company utilizes a team approach to investment management. The team approach provides for thorough and effective training for portfolio managers and traders. As a rule, Wyeth Company hires only highly skilled professionals with strong investment backgrounds. Investment decisions are made across all portfolios with similar investment guidelines. Portfolio managers perform their own research and are responsible for particular industries. Cross-training occurs as portfolio managers rotate across industry specialties and investment strategy is discussed daily. Traders are an integral part of the investment process. They continually communicate with the portfolio managers in matters regarding current investment strategies. The daily interaction and discussion among the professionals enables each individual of the investment team to be well versed in the techniques and strategies used in the value equity process. The firm encourages and financially supports after-work attendance for professional programs, such as CFAs and MBAs.

Example B4-3

Many of Bierstadt, Inc., Advisory Group's investment professionals are "home grown" talent. Many of our portfolio managers have worked their way up through the ranks of our Research Department, often spending a large portion of their careers as an analyst or associate portfolio manager before assuming management duties for specific portfolios. The training that is provided to all of our investment professionals consists of a program that begins by selecting experienced, talented professionals and brings them through varying stages of "trainee" to "staff" to "senior team members" according to their individual talents and desires. Our research analysts either have earned CFA designations prior to hire or enroll in a program to earn the designation at such time as we extend an offer of employment. Several of our portfolio managers and our Director of Research teach courses for individuals preparing to take CFA examinations.

Example B4-4

Internal training procedures for portfolio managers, traders, and research analysts at O'Keefe Guarantee might best be described as analogous to an apprenticeship program. Unless hired at a very high level of experience and proficiency, professionals new to the Company or the position will work closely with an experienced colleague. As levels of knowledge and proficiency are demonstrated, responsibilities are increased until the professional is operating autonomously. The length or formality of the training will vary with the complexity of the position and the individual's ability. This individualized approach ensures that all new professionals are thoroughly grounded in all aspects of their position and that level of responsibility follows demonstrated proficiency.

Comments:

Several common approaches are employed by firms when discussing professional development.

The first approach is the "we are all seasoned professionals and formal training is not necessary" approach. This approach again highlights the distinction between large and small firms. Remington & Associates, for example, only has five professionals and only one was not experienced when joining the firm. Wyeth, a fairly large firm, also emphasizes the general rule of hiring skilled professionals. In contrast, Bierstadt discusses training after the initial selection of "experienced, talented professionals."

The second approach is the "we keep sharp by interacting as a team" approach. Remington, as a small firm, emphasizes the value of teamwork, as does Wyeth. This is all well and good, but doesn't really address training per se.

The third approach is the "apprenticeship" approach. Whenever I read this, I cannot help but think back to the guilds in Renaissance Europe. Apprenticeship for professionals can take the form of (1) working closely with the master craftsman, as at O'Keefe Guarantee; (2) rotation of assignments, as at Wyeth Company; or (3) formally working their way up through stages of development, as at Bierstadt, Inc.

The final approach is the use of "outside resources," such as MBA or CFA training at Wyeth and Bierstadt.

All four approaches should be part of the training and development program at money management firms. However, none of the examples listed really answers the question satisfactorily. Firms should emphasize that education and the honing of one's craft is never really completed for any professional. Active participation at seminars, conferences, etc., should be required for all professionals in addition to internal programs instituted by the firm.

The really forward-thinking firm will tie in these formal training activities to the integration of new ideas into the investment process.

B5. Please describe your compensation and program with respect to keeping and motivating key professionals.

Example B5-1

Remington & Associates pays its professionals very competitive salaries, a full benefit package, plus bonus based on the firm's success. Evaluation is informal, but constant, as "the proof is in the pudding." Remington's history of superior returns is the direct result of the firm's superior investment staff.

Equity ownership is available and has been distributed to all investment professionals. Further details on firm ownership distribution will be disclosed at an appropriate time, if necessary.

Example B5-2

Portfolio managers at Bierstadt, Inc., are compensated with base salaries comparable to those in the upper 10% of the industry. The bonuses of our portfolio managers are calculated based upon the performance of accounts they manage relative to the market and relative to the performance of their peers in widely accepted relative performance universes. Performance below the median does not earn a bonus. The bonus can increase salary by as much as 100% for consistently superior performance. The multiplier used to calculate the bonus is designed to provide the maximum reward for consistently superior performance year after year rather than one year of stellar performance. Our analysts' bonuses are calculated based upon the strength of their buy and sell recommendations. They too may receive additional compensation up to 100% of their salaries.

Example B5-3

Base salaries are established by Wyeth's management at competitive levels to attract and maintain the best professional talent. In addition, an incentive bonus equal to a significant percentage of the firm's pre-tax profits is paid out each year to the firm's employees based upon the *individual's performance and the profitability of the firm.* The bonus generally represents a sizeable amount relative to base salaries, and when added to salaries, results in highly attractive levels of total cash compensation for the firm's professionals. Every employee is in the bonus pool. This approach instills a strong sense of commitment on the part of every employee and a stake in the success of the firm. In addition, in January of 1992 the firm's management, working with its parent, put in place a Long-Term Performance Plan designed to provide Wyeth Company professionals with a 20% participation in the market value of the firm. Equity ownership is determined by the Management Committee and is distributed to key professionals on the basis of their long-term commitment to the firm and their contribution to successful investment management.

Example B5-4

Sargent Trust has implemented both financial and nonfinancial incentives to assure that key professionals are properly rewarded and professionally challenged. As a package, these incentives insure that key professionals remain at Sargent Trust. These incentives include:

- Compensation: Sargent Trust awards bonuses based on both investment and professional performance. Portfolio performance is measured relative to the market and competitive portfolios with similar objectives. In addition, Sargent Trust issues incentive shares based on individual performance but distributed based on company performance. Incentive shares ensure that investment professionals contribute to the overall profitability of the firm and maintain a team work ethic. Sargent Trust's total compensation is competitive with other investment firms.

- Employee ownership: Sargent Trust is owned by over 200 of its employees, including investment professionals and senior management. This ownership inspires an entrepreneurial enthusiasm within the company. Professionals making key contributions to the organization are provided with the opportunity to buy stock.

- Extensive resources, research support, and systems: Investment professionals have access to the resources and research they need to make well-informed decisions on a timely basis. Also, Sargent Trust has invested in extensive information systems to provide efficient, up-to-date access to both internal and external research, investment analytics, and market data. This provides a streamlined network over which the Sargent Trust professional can formulate decisions, execute transactions, process trades, and monitor results.

Comments:

An effective compensation program should incorporate several elements.

First, individuals should be compensated with a full benefit package and a reasonable annual salary.

Second, bonuses should be tied to both individual performance and performance of the firm. Professionals should be rewarded for adding value individually, but should benefit as the whole group benefits. It makes no sense to talk about teamwork and then to reward professionals only on some measure of individual efforts.

Third, professionals are more highly motivated when they are given a piece of the action. Otherwise, they will feel and act like hired guns—even if expensive hired guns.

Fourth, all people want to work in a stimulating and fun working environment. No amount of money can compensate for a miserable work life.

Remington & Associates appears to emphasize the success of the firm rather than success of the individual in determining compensation. This makes sense given the size of the firm.

In contrast, Bierstadt, Inc., strives to pay people well (i.e., upper 10% in the industry) but does not appear to offer ownership or incentives based on the firm's overall success. Also, the compensation appears to be based on a quantitative formula and incorporates little regarding qualitative contributions. This is quite interesting because, in example B3-4, Bierstadt talks about the team approach to portfolio management. Are the financial incentives lined up to be consistent with the investment decision-making process?

Wyeth seems to incorporate the right incentives in the first three elements. Individuals are paid a high base salary and incentives are tied to the firm's profitability and equity position. If the compensation is distributed fairly, it makes one wonder why there was turnover (see example B1-2). Perhaps the working environment was less than desirable.

I really like Sargent Trust's response. Professionals appear to be compensated for individual contributions to investment portfolios and to other areas. An incentive to contribute to organizational success is present and, finally, Sargent provides systems support that will allow the professional to do a better job. Few firms talk about nonfinancial incentives when responding to this question.

B6. Please describe the qualifications you seek when hiring professionals.

Example B6-1

Wyeth Company hires the most qualified and experienced investment professionals available, with a special emphasis on research abilities. Technical expertise, a successful track record, and high levels of education are criteria in selecting professionals. Typically, investment professionals will have at least five years of working experience and an advanced degree such as an MBAs, CFA, etc. However, Wyeth Company also evaluates the individual's ability to work effectively in a team structure. This is in direct contrast to other portfolio management firms that employ a "star" system of investment management. We believe this is a distinct advantage to our clients.

Example B6-2

When Bierstadt, Inc., hires portfolio managers, we are typically interested in highly experienced investment professionals who have specific backgrounds in the style and approach in which the vacancy occurs. More often than not, we promote our most promising investment professionals who have demonstrated to us that they have the talent and experience to succeed.

All of our analysts are expected to earn Chartered Financial Analyst designations. Our traders have had previous institutional trading experience and our systems professionals have had previous experience in investment-related systems development.

Comments:

Qualifications of new employees should include elements of high technical competence, personal integrity, and professional demeanor. Both Wyeth and Bierstadt do a pretty nice job of describing the kind of individuals that they seek from a technical viewpoint. Although Bierstadt mentions that they look for people with the ability to work as a team, both firms could do a better job of emphasizing the nontechnical aspects of potential hires.

Of course, if firms hire well, they should be able to promote from within. Bierstadt makes this point well.

C. Product Philosophy and Investment Process

Questions on product philosophy and investment process are open-ended and provide the investment advisor an opportunity to strut and crow. The successful investment advisor will capture the imagination of the investor through cogency and consistency of philosophy, strategy, and implementation of trades.

The story should be believable and, indeed, substantiated by superior returns.

C1. Please describe your investment philosophy for the subject product. Why do you believe your process will be successful in the future? Please provide any evidence or research that supports this belief.

Example C1-1

Remington & Associates believes superior long-term results can best be earned by consistently achieving superior short-term performance.

To meet this objective, Remington has a value-oriented approach to its portfolio management.

- First, we **screen** our universe for stocks using several **relative value criteria**,

- However, no purchase is made unless there is a **catalyst happening within the company** that will change the perceived value of the stock.

- Next, we **set price targets** averaging a 50% return for each stock over two years, and **actively trade** around that "trendline."

- We sell stocks when price targets are achieved, when the catalyst is spent or disappears, or if fundamentals deteriorate.

The firm establishes a core of holdings, with portfolios normally holding between 40 and 50 issues. The average market capitalization of stocks held ranges from $2 to $6 billion.

Although past performance is no guarantee of future results, Remington & Associates has a proven, excellent performance record that has beaten the S&P 500 in 12 of the last 13 calendar years. In addition, the performance record ranks highly when compared to peer managers in consultant universes. This investment process and approach has been successful in the past during both rising and falling markets and is expected to be so in the future.

Example C1-2

The Wyeth Company believes that we can outperform the market and our competition with lower risk by uniquely combining investment disciplines with the fundamental judgment of seasoned professionals. We believe that our value equity process will be successful in the future because the investment process is disciplined, well-defined, and consistently applied. Our use of "value catalysts" greatly enhances the timeliness of purchases, and our disciplined diversification parameters among major sectors control risk. These two steps are unique to our process and we believe will consistently allow us to outperform the competition and the averages with low risk.

Example C1-3

Bierstadt, Inc., provides active management of emerging, growth stock portfolios using an approach that focuses upon growth trend analysis to identify and overweight rapidly growing industries and upon fundamental analysis and valuation techniques for individual stock selection. We believe our process will continue to be successful for these three reasons: our unique approach, our outstanding research, and our stability.

Our top-down approach is a highly differentiating feature, as a preponderance of growth stock managers have a bottom-up orientation. We believe that theme, sector, and industry analyses demonstrate the opportunities for greatest potential growth within our forecasted economic environment.

Our research capabilities have contributed to our success and will continue to do so. At a time when many investment management firms as well as Wall Street brokerage houses are curtailing their research efforts, Bierstadt, Inc., remains committed to a strong research effort. This is particularly essential to a small-capitalization investment approach. To accurately identify emerging companies that will prosper and grow is a difficult endeavor that requires a constant refreshing of the investment universe, a familiarity with the venture capital and new issues pipeline, and ongoing analysis of changing developments in smaller growth companies. One cannot rely exclusively on external research for ideas in these emerging sectors. Our Research Department's equity analysts follow over 1,000 such companies on an ongoing basis, providing first-hand knowledge with critical timeliness and, ultimately, contributing to consistently superior performance.

Another distinguishing characteristic of Bierstadt, Inc., that will continue to play a role in our success is the stability created through our ownership structure. We benefit from the resources available through ownership by Bierstadt-Stuart Financial Corporation, such as research dollars, investment in technology, and other capital. While we operate as an independent investment firm and thereby preserve the flexibility and cohesiveness necessary for effective decision making, we are not plagued with the financial limitations that oftentimes can be debilitating for small investment firms.

Example C1-4

Investment Philosophy

The Premier Equity Discipline of Sargent Trust is an innovative investment approach combining active management with quantitative risk control. We believe that intensive analysis of small-cap companies will identify securities that will outperform in the future. We also believe that structuring active picks within a risk-controlled portfolio will deliver consistent value-added over and above an index.

The objective of the Premier Equity Discipline is to earn excess return from actively selected securities while maintaining similar industry weights, cross-industry characteristics, and return volatility to a client-specified benchmark. Special care is used to provide a liquid portfolio.

Future Success of Sargent Trust Investment Process

Sargent Trust makes a major commitment to resources by reinvesting a significant portion of our annual revenues. We constantly enhance our systems technology and strengthen our worldwide research team. These resources support the investment process.

Sargent Trust has developed its own global research effort to support our investment management business. We have 65 domestic and 25 international equity analysts, who follow a "bottom-up" investment approach. This research team, located in 10 offices around the world, analyzes over 7,000 companies worldwide. Analysts rely on direct management contact, competitive environment analysis, and input from both company suppliers and customers for information. We generate over 65% of our research internally. Moreover, Sargent Trust research capabilities continue to grow, from 70 analysts in 1992 to 90 in 1994.

A unique feature of Sargent Trust's research process is that its research analysts actually make buy and sell decisions for their own industry mutual funds (35 Premier Funds). The relative performance of these funds comprises a major part of the analysts' annual compensation and is a major determinant with respect to career growth.

Our research effort is enhanced by a comprehensive network of resources, including an extensive library, advanced information systems, and sophisticated trading capabilities. The unique combination of people and resources has allowed Sargent Trust to produce outstanding results in the past and supports our expectation of superior results in the future.

Future Success of Premier Equity

The historical breadth and consistency of value-added from Sargent Trust's fundamental research (the source of value-added for the Premier Equity Discipline) and the rigor of the quantitative risk-control procedures give us confidence that the Premier Equity process will continue to add value in the future.

Diversified at two levels, the investment process protects its portfolios from the effects of sectors or investment styles moving in or out of vogue in the future. First, the Premier Equity process constructs and maintains portfolios to have fundamental characteristics (Market Cap, P/E, Yield, etc.) and industry weights consistent with the chosen benchmark. This neutral exposure ensures that the returns to the Premier Equity portfolio will neither benefit nor be penalized as returns to these different characteristics change in the future.

Second, the source of value-added for the Premier Equity process, qualitative fundamental stock selection, is well diversified across many analysts. Rather than relying on a single valuation process or quantitative model that implicitly assumes that past value-added of some sector(s) or style(s) will persist into the future, Sargent Trust's analysts select stocks based on their own unique valuation processes. This is a forward-looking, dynamic process that has consistently provided value-added across both time and industries. We have conducted extensive research documenting the power and consistency of our analysts' stock picks.

Further, the consistency of value-added in the diversified Premier Equity Small-Cap portfolio (value-added in 85% of quarters) has been virtually the same regardless of the general direction of the market or the relative performance of large- and small-cap stocks. This is due to the combined success of our risk-control and stock selection processes.

The breadth and consistency of value-added from Sargent Trust's research, in combination with rigorous risk-control procedures, gives us confidence in the future success of the Premier Equity Small-Cap Discipline.

Comments:

When writing the response to this question, the investment advisor should recall Composition 101. The responses should be separated into Introduction, Theme, and Conclusion. The introduction should tie into the reason the firm was created by the principals and lead into the themes. The conclusion should tie it all together with emphasis on future performance. The text need not be long to satisfy proper form.

Remington talks about having "a value-oriented approach." This is not a philosophy, it's a statement. What is Remington's definition of value-added? Why is this important? What evidence is there to support this philosophy? What is Remington's real commitment? All of these questions can be answered succinctly and tie to the years of meaningful experience of the principals. If the principals are disciples of Graham and Dodd they should say so and point to the evidence for validation.

Even given my criticisms of Remington regarding their incomplete responses, they do list the themes underlying their philosophy: (1) look for relative value, (2) look for companies that have undergone change, (3) establish intrinsic value along trendlines, and (4) sell stocks against those trendlines or when the catalyst disappears. In conclusion, they cite the usual connection between anticipated future results and past results. They end with a nice statement that adds integrity: the process has worked in rising and falling markets. Remington's response would be better if they stated why this was true and provide numbers in user-friendly form to support the statement.

I have included the Wyeth Company example for two reasons. First, we shall see that the investment process is very similar to that of Remington. Second, when compared to the last two examples and even to Remington, their discussion dramatically fails to provide insights into their raison d'etre.

Wyeth believes this and believes that, but why? For all the meaning that is conveyed, Wyeth might as well substitute the terms "apple pie," "mom," and "baseball" for their descriptors, "lower risk," "investment discipline," and "fundamental judgment." Introducing "value catalysts" without explaining their significance is sloppy. There is no philosophy imparted here, only gobbledy-gook.

Bierstadt provides a good example of summarizing their philosophy. They introduce the subject by stating up front their investment tenets: active management, top-down trends, stocks exhibiting growth in growth industries, companies having fundamental and intrinsic value. Their response would be complete if they had added a sentiment to the effect that "our research shows that companies exhibiting these growth characteristics have proven to add value provided that they are not overpriced."

Bierstadt couples their philosophy to their process by stating their competitive advantages: unique approach, research, and stability.

The body of their response includes elaborating on three advantages. Each advantage stands on its own. The focus on top-down provides a consistency and discipline that most stock pickers do not have. Research on individual companies means that the best companies can be selected to support the top-down theme. Finally, a stable organization will support the research efforts without the portfolio managers worrying about such mundane things as financial strength. Although the connection of each advantage to a broader whole could be made more explicit, the careful reader will pick up on the interaction.

Sargent Trust employs a much different kind of philosophy than Bierstadt, though the themes are clear. First, Bierstadt relies solely on superior company identification, while ignoring investment themes and sector bets in order to construct a portfolio close to the benchmark. Second, the manager is quantitatively driven.

In the body of the response, Sargent chose to explicitly answer the question on future success. Sargent focuses on the reinvestment of revenues into research and resources. They also refer to the implementation of strategy through the independent industry mutual funds. In other words, the portfolios are actually a composite of discrete industry portfolios that parallel those run for other clients. The astute reader will understand that Sargent is creating this product by leveraging up the efforts that have gone into creating the Premier funds. By not making thematic or sector bets, and as long as the Premier funds span the market universe, there is no need for extra work and cost to Sargent in constructing this portfolio. This is a pretty piece of work of product extension by Sargent.

In the last section, Sargent gets into the crux of the philosophy and its success. The risk-control and diversification discussion makes intuitive sense and would appeal to clients who want the advantage of bottom-up research without the volatility relative to the benchmarks. Their approach is unique and would likely add a new dimension to the typical manager in client's portfolios. Research, research, and research is the common theme and cannot be stated too often.

The following statement is wonderful and right on target to convince the potential client that undoubtedly value will be added in the future.

> This is a forward-looking, dynamic process that has consistently provided value-added across both time and industries. We have conducted extensive research documenting the power and consistency of our analysts' stock picks.

Finally, the last paragraph talking about breadth, consistency, and risk-control brings all the themes together succinctly. Sargent's business strategists, portfolio managers, and RFP writers all get an A+++.

C2. Please describe your decision-making process. How does your firm implement its philosophy (e.g., buy/sell decisions)?

Example C2-1

The focus of the implementation process of Remington & Associates' philosophy is bottom-up. The stock selection decision begins with the individual portfolio manager or analyst, who is in continual contact with sources of ideas. These sources include Wall Street contacts, company managers, and an extensive in-house research database. Normally, 70% of our research ideas are generated internally and 30% outside the firm.

At formal, weekly meetings, and through continual, informal communication, investment ideas are discussed by the five investment professionals at Remington & Associates. Stocks come to the forefront when catalysts are present and provide a change in perception. These catalysts include changes in company management, new products or technologies, and consolidation, acquisitions, or divestitures. All portfolios are managed on a team basis so that all portfolios look the same.

The criteria for stocks purchased are a good balance sheet, strong cash flow, a price/earnings multiple less than that of the market or competitive stocks, low cash-flow multiples, being a leader in its industry, and a lack of recognition among institutional investors.

Conversely, positions are reduced if prices exceed target trendlines. They are sold outright when price targets are achieved, when the catalyst no longer exists, or if the fundamentals do not evolve as previously expected. Recent portfolio sales turnover has averaged 100%.

The universe of securities from which Remington & Associates draws investment ideas is determined by valuation levels and is usually about 600 names. The core list generally numbers 300. Portfolio mangers develop close relationships with each of these companies through personal visits, either through New York meetings or direct company visits. Portfolios generally consist of between 40 and 50 issues.

If no opportunities exist after sales proceeds have been raised, cash equivalents may prove to be the best investment alternative. However, the normal stance for the firm is to be fully invested, and cash reserves do not normally exceed 10% of the portfolio.

Example C2-2

Wyeth Company's value equity strategy focuses on low P/E and/or low price/cash-flow stocks and is designed to provide both competitive performance and lower than market risk. Our value screens select the lowest quartile (25%) in the stock universe based on P/E and/or price/cash flow ratios. The screens are flexible in terms of capitalizations of $300 million and up. The portfolio management team then uses quantitative and qualitative screens to identify candidates that generate free cash flow and to eliminate financially weak companies by looking at factors such as interest coverage ratios.

Wyeth Company must be able to find several proven "value catalysts" that will cause the stock price to appreciate sooner rather than later before we can buy a stock. These catalysts include: stock buybacks, management ownership, asset restructuring, discount to private market value, positive earnings trends, and above-average dividend yield. Several of these catalysts must be present for us to consider buying the stock.

After the screening process, including the "value catalyst" test, we typically have a focus list of approximately 100-150 stocks. At this point, we begin fundamental research by using a variety of information sources (e.g., financial statements, Wall Street research, periodicals, competitors, and customers) to learn the industry and company dynamics. We basically obtain a "bull" and "bear" story on the stock and then contact the company directly to learn about their view of the fundamentals. If the company dynamics are positive, we then write a brief research report and review some technical characteristics. The team then meets to discuss the merits of the investment.

Wyeth Company utilizes a team approach to all investment management, including the development of overall investment policy and research analysis. No single portfolio manager is solely responsible for a particular account. Investment decisions are made by the portfolio management team, headed by Winslow Homer, across all accounts. The well-defined value process described above is what drives the construction of our portfolios, and therefore no individual portfolio manager has any latitude to deviate from the team's strategy. Portfolios may differ based on client objectives. However, fully discretionary, value equity accounts with identical guidelines will have similar holdings, and are included in our value equity composite.

Sell Discipline

Wyeth Company believes that one of the most important ways to reduce risk in a portfolio is by having rigorous sell disciplines. The following four factors influence the sell decision:

1. Valuation

    • P/E and/or price/cash-flow ratio rises above market levels

    • Stock price rises above private transaction value

2. Diversification

    • 5% maximum position in any one stock (3% in practice)

    • Sector weighting limits relative to S&P 500

3. Change in Fundamentals

    • Company fails financial, operating, or "value catalyst" tests

4. Price Action

    • Stock price increases over 50% over a six-month period

The firm would not deviate from its well-defined disciplines under any circumstances.

Investment Process Summary

Our process is unique in two ways. The use of "value catalysts" helps in the timeliness of purchases, i.e., the value of the stock is about to be recognized; and the diversification process reduces risk.

Example C2-3

Outlined below are the stages of Bierstadt's investment process.

Stage I.   **Analyze current growth trends.**

Evaluate specific social, political, and economic factors driving change in the U.S. economy.

Determine secular forces influencing these changes—their importance and longevity as well as their potential impact (both positive and negative) on growth trends.

Stage II.   **Analyze current growth industries** (determination of winners and losers based upon the growth trend analysis).

Identify specific industries offering the best investment prospects.

Determine industries that involve exceptionally high risk and avoid them.

Stage III. Analyze growth stocks.

Consider input from internal and external research.

Evaluate company characteristics as described.

Use proprietary valuation screens to further evaluate specific stocks.

Develop Emerging Growth Tier Chart.

Stage IV. Formulate emerging growth portfolios.

Construct and actively manage portfolios in accordance with client guidelines and structure established by Emerging Growth Tier Chart.

Stage V. Portfolio review.

Review portfolios on an ongoing basis to ensure compliance with strategy as represented in Tier Chart.

Review portfolios on an ongoing basis to ensure compliance with client objectives.

Review portfolios with clients quarterly and annually, or as requested by the client.

Accounts are reviewed on a daily basis by the investment team. In addition, Claude Monet, Chief Investment Officer of Bierstadt, Inc., Growth Spectrum Advisors, reviews portfolios weekly to ensure compliance with our Tier Board structure. When policy has been set, the portfolio managers may not deviate from our objectives or hold securities that have not been approved for the "Tier Board." Portfolios may differ slightly due to client-imposed guidelines.

Example C2-4

Implementation by O'Keefe of the Systematic Equity philosophy is described below. We *do not deviate from its disciplines.*

Since we generally run portfolios fully invested, decisions to buy and sell stocks are made simultaneously using a computer-based optimizer.

The information required by the optimizer is:

1. A universe of appropriate mid-cap companies both to act as an approved list and to provide industry weight targets. If a client has a particular benchmark in mind, the industry weights from the benchmark are used.

2. The relative attractiveness (alphas) of the stocks in the universe. We have a proprietary technique for deriving these, but they are essentially based on the long-term fundamental prospects of each of the companies.

3. The relative riskiness of the stocks.

4. Prospective transaction costs.

5. The target characteristics of/constraints on the portfolio. In the case of Mid-Cap Growth for example, it would include parameters such as a desired average market cap.

The optimizer considers these things simultaneously to construct a new portfolio with the best set of risk/return characteristics.

Once the portfolio is established, the optimization process is repeated periodically and trades are made only when they will enhance risk/return characteristics net of prospective transaction costs. Resulting turnover is on the order of 25% annually.

Comments:

Obviously, the investment process must be consistent with the responses on organization and philosophy in order to be considered legitimate and to have integrity. Remington introduces the concepts of "relative value criteria" and "catalysts" in their discourse on philosophy (i.e., example C1-1). The description of the investment process gives these concepts meaning by stating the proxies for value (e.g., cash flow, P/E.) and catalysts (changes in company management, new products, etc.). The sell discipline is laid out and, as it should be, is the flip side of the buy decision.

Remington discusses the universe and portfolio construction. A characteristic of most small firms that have no institutional history distinct from the founding principals, Remington's decision-making process is less formal. However, the reader has been provided a clear picture of how decisions are made and why.

I encourage the reader to review the Wyeth Company example (example C2-2) and then re-read Remington's description (example C2-1). Interestingly, the Wyeth investment process is almost identical to that of Remington: examining fundamental values, looking for catalysts, utilizing company research, etc. Yet, although the philosophy presented by Wyeth was very incomplete in example C1-2, the description of the actual process is excellent. In other words, the "what" is better articulated than the "why."

Wyeth explains in detail how the screens are applied, which catalysts are important, the role of fundamental research, the importance of teamwork, the specific guidelines behind sell decisions and, finally, the unique attributes of their approach. The strategy makes sense, and appears to be rigorous in fact and not just in words. Certainly, although the similarities to Remington are striking, the formality of the process is clearly better defined.

The investment process description of Bierstadt, Inc., is fairly mechanistic. The steps are outlined, but the reader could not possibly feel as though he or she is being "talked to." The content is good, but Bierstadt should be less rigid in its description. Perhaps an example walking through the steps of analysis would have been enlightening.

Being a more quantitative shop, O'Keefe Guarantee has an easier time precisely articulating the process of making investment decisions. O'Keefe makes maximum use of this advantage by being succinct and articulate. They list the inputs of the optimizer and the outputs. Their highlighted statement that disciplines are never deviated from is a nice touch.

O'Keefe does have a fatal flaw, which becomes apparent to the careful reader. They do not discuss the stocks that are "appropriate" and comprise their "approved list."

C3. Please describe how your portfolio is constructed.

Example C3-1

Wyeth Company utilizes a team approach to all investment management. No single portfolio manager is solely responsible for any particular account. Each portfolio benefits from the same, proven quantitative disciplines and seasoned judgment of the team. A single stock may not comprise more than 5% of the portfolio, and usually averages 1-1/2% to 2%. Individual stock positions are the result of bottom-up stock selection combining the screens and the judgment of the portfolio team, with each portfolio manager having a certain industry/sector expertise. The specific weight is a function of how well a stock fits our value criteria. Each position is bought for all accounts with the same percentage weighting, unless a client objective stipulates otherwise (i.e., South Africa-free). Portfolios must have representation in four major sectors: Capital Goods, Basic Materials, Consumer Related, and Interest-Rate Sensitive. The weightings in these sectors must be +/- 50% of the respective S&P weights. For fully discretionary accounts, capitalization ranges are generally not limited. We are able, however, to comply with restricted capitalization range requests if a client so desires.

Example C3-2

Trend and Industry Analysis

The initial phase of Bierstadt's investment process involves identification and evaluation of growth trends. To do this, we analyze specific social, political, and economic factors driving change in the U.S. economy. Based upon this analysis, we determine the secular forces that are influencing and shaping these changes. We examine the importance and longevity of these secular forces as well as their potential impact (positive and negative) on growth trends. We believe that currently the four sectors of the economy promising greatest growth potential are technology, healthcare, distinct consumer niches, and business services.

Following our growth trend analysis, we analyze growth industries. We determine which industries will benefit from specific growth trends we have identified, as well as those that will suffer. We avoid the industries that represent exceptionally high risk.

Fundamental Analysis

Following our growth industry analysis, we analyze and evaluate growth stocks within industries promising the most favorable risk/reward expectations. Companies are first evaluated for the presence of specific fundamental characteristics we believe are critically important:

- Projected annual earnings growth of 80% or more over the next three to five years based on our own research analysis;

- High relative return on stockholders' equity;

- Low debt to total capitalization.

Above and beyond this traditional fundamental analysis, we believe that our research can add the most value by "going beyond the numbers." In our opinion, it's crucial to get to know a company's management in order to examine whether the individuals are demonstrating a degree of urgency in meeting growth and profit objectives, whether they are exercising proper control of expenses, debt and margins, whether they have successful previous track records, and whether their future success is tied to that of the company through a proper compensation structure.

Additionally, by meeting management and visiting companies directly, we can learn their true competitive posture. Among other factors, we are interested in having the following questions answered to our satisfaction. Are there any new competitors or replacement products foreseen by management but not yet known by the investment community? Is there a sound strategy for combating current and future sources of competition? Does the company have an edge, either through quality or cost of focus? Every stock considered for our emerging growth portfolios must be appealing on a fundamental basis before we proceed with our valuation analysis.

Screening Criteria and Structure

Individual securities must meet our screening criteria to be eligible for further analysis. These criteria are earnings growth and annual revenues. Companies must have annual revenues of $200 million to $1 billion and three- to five-year earnings growth rates of 80-90% to be candidates for our tier chart (see Table 1).

TABLE 1. TIER CHART

	Technology	Healthcare	Consumer	Business Services
Tier #1, Each Name 3.5% - 6% of the Portfolio	Cisco Systems Policy Management			
Tier #2, Each Name 2% - 3.5% of the Portfolio	BMC Software, Inc. HBO & Co. Legent Corp. Novell Inc. Parametric Tech. Wellfleet Comm.	Haemonetrics Corp.	Bombay Co. Inc. Cracker Barrel	Multimedia Inc. Olsten Corp.
Tier #3, Each Name 0.50% - 2% of the Portfolio	Chipcom Corp. Informix Corp. Linear Technology Maxim Integrated Read-Rite Corp. Silicon Graphics Inc. Sybase Inc. Synoptics Comm. Syquest Technology Tellabs Inc.	Alza Corp. Applied Bioscience Chiron Corp. Datascope Corp. Forest Laboratories Gensia Pharm. Genzyme Corp. Healthcare Compare Healthsouth Rehab. Lifecore Biomedical U.S. Surgical Corp. Ventritex Inc. Visx Inc.	Au Bon Pain Inc. Belo (A.H.) Corp. Brinker Int'l Inc. Buffets Inc. Compusa Inc. Int'l Game Tech. Jan Bell Marketing Jones Apparel Luxottica Group Marvel Ent. Phillips-Van Heusen QVC Network Inc.	Amtech Corp. BE Aerospace Inc. Catalina Marketing Gentex Corp. Idexx Labs Inc. Information Res. Octel Comm. Paychex Inc. Sensormatic Elect. Simpson Industries Superior Industries

We prefer to screen securities by revenues and earnings growth for several reasons. Measurable increases in sales and earnings are often the best available indicators of a company's growth potential. Capitalization size is much more volatile. Investor sentiment may take an individual equity issue from a small-capitalization range to large-capitalization and back again in very short periods of time. Measures of profitability are avoided, since they would exclude companies not currently profitable; and yet these companies may represent the best profit opportunities longer term.

We have developed an investment tool, the tier chart, to structure portfolios. Our current tier chart demonstrates the emphasis we place on the industries that include the most promising growth trends: Technology,

Healthcare, Consumer Services, and Business Services. Vertically, on the left side of the tier chart, appear tier #1, tier #2, and tier #3. These tiers divide stocks according to their relative attractiveness, and those securities are held in differing percentages within the portfolio accordingly. Each tier #1 stock will represent from 3.5 to 6% of the holdings within a portfolio; each tier #2 stock, 2 to 3.5% of a portfolio; and each tier #3 stock, 0.50 to 2% of a portfolio.

Our tier chart also plays a role in our sell discipline. A stock that appears in tier #3 may have been a tier #1 stock at one time and subsequently been downgraded to a tier #3 stock as part of our strategy to phase it out of the portfolio. Stocks are generally sold because of valuation changes caused by appreciation or changes in fundamentals or some combination of the two. Specifically, sales may occur if a stock's relative value diminishes due to a negative change in fundamentals with or without a price change, or if a stock's relative value diminishes due to appreciation without a change in fundamentals.

Valuation System

In addition to the fundamental characteristics that should be present, we further screen companies through a proprietary valuation system we have developed. We monitor relative, estimated three- to five–year earnings growth rates and p/e ratios, and divide one by the other to create our Valuation Index. The higher the growth rate per p/e ratio, the more potentially attractive the investment, and vice-versa. Every "buy" candidate is examined in this fashion, as are all securities in existing portfolios.

Comments:

Assessing the rigor applied to portfolio construction is a significant activity for staff, consultants, and board members who are serious about hiring exceptional managers. Both these examples articulate well the portfolio's construction in terms of security weights, sector control, and consistency of themes. A well-thought-out plan for portfolio construction can make the difference between managers who win accounts and those who do not.

C4. If securities in the portfolio have particular characteristics, please describe them.

Example C4-1

Securities in Bierstadt's portfolios are distinguished by particular characteristics. Earnings growth is a critically important characteristic. We are only interested in companies which will deliver earnings growth of 80% or greater over the coming three to five years based upon our own analysis. A high return on stockholders' equity is another important characteristic. In addition, we are interested in companies that are dominant or leaders within their own industries and that are the low-cost providers of a product or service. The company must also be committed to research and development aimed at maintaining its dominance. Finally, management must have a proven track record, appropriate compensation structure, and a stake in the company.

Typical portfolio characteristics:

Median market capitalization	$1 billion
Median annual revenues	$500 million
Median earnings growth rate	85.0%
Median 1995 P/E Ratio	25.0
Median return on equity	20.0
Debt to total cap	7.5

Comments:

Again, Bierstadt explains very nicely the kinds of securities that will be in the portfolio. If the kinds of security characteristics fluctuate in the portfolios, they should do so because of explicit strategies and processes employed by the managers. In today's world, plan sponsors want to know what they are getting in the portfolio from their external investment advisors.

C5. Please describe the universe of securities in which you operate in terms of market capitalization and liquidity.

Example C5-1

Market Capitalization

There are no explicit boundaries on market caps for individual securities in the Sargent Trust's Premier Equity process. We construct a portfolio in such a way that the weighted average capitalization is consistent with that of the chosen benchmark. Further, we constrain the portfolio to ensure that the distribution of market caps of assets in the portfolio is consistent with that of the benchmark. As a result, the portfolio's market cap exposure is consistent with its benchmark.

Liquidity

Liquidity is a central element of the proper construction of small-cap portfolios. Liquidity control in the Premier Equity Discipline is of two parts. First, the selection of the top 25 holdings in each select industry mutual fund as the starting universe for the Premier Equity process provides an implicit liquidity filter. Stocks will not be in this list if they are not tradable. Second, we limit the maximum weight of any stock in a Premier Equity portfolio to one day's average trading volume per $250 million of portfolio value (a $250 million Premier Equity portfolio will weight holdings in such a way that each position represents less than its average daily trading volume).

As a result, Premier Equity portfolios possess excellent relative liquidity. Average bid-ask spreads are lower and average daily dollar volumes are higher than those of the benchmark.

Comments:

Sargent Trust appropriately states that market capitalization is dependent upon client benchmark objectives. Of course, this does not preclude the advantage of stating explicitly the capitalization requirements if those requirements are relevant to the investment process. Liquidity should always be explicitly addressed and, if necessary, trading guidelines established to reflect liquidity constraints.

C6. Please describe what market conditions would favor the subject product's strategy.

Example C6-1

Remington & Associates expects its equity investment process to do well in all market environments. As the year-by-year return numbers indicate, we have outperformed the S&P 500 in 12 of the last 13 years. This period includes both rising and falling markets.

Example C6-2

Wyeth Company value approach expects to outperform the averages in down markets and to perform in line with the averages in up markets. This performance profile allows us to outperform the market and competition over complete market cycles with below-average risk.

The value equity product is expected to outperform the market as the economy emerges from a recession and underperform the market when the economy is going into a recession. However, the price/free cash-flow analysis of a company prevents Wyeth Company from buying stocks whose issuers are financially weak. We tend to outperform other value managers in a recession for this reason.

Example C6-3

Bierstadt, Inc.

Generally speaking, the strategy of Bierstadt is favored during bull market phases in which economic growth is moderate to strong. However, in bear markets or down markets, we typically perform well relative to other small to mid-cap managers.

Comments:

With respect to this question, the investor is interested in hearing two things. First, does the product perform during all periods. If so, why? If not, why not? If droughts occur, it is up to the advisor to convince the prospective client that the expectation of extra return achieved during good performing periods is enough to compensate for the underperformance during other periods.

Second, what objective proof can the advisor provide in stating his case?

Remington is good at providing evidence that the process works in rising and falling markets, but they do not say why it works. Is there an option with Remington's process to take bigger bets in order to achieve higher long-term returns, even though there may be more years of underperformance?

In contrast to Remington, Wyeth mentions that value may underperform the market (i.e., growth stocks) during new recessionary periods. They also explain how this trend is mitigated by avoiding financially weak securities. Of course, their argument would be stronger if they actually presented data to support their case.

Bierstadt's response neither provides proof nor explains why the results occur as they do. Their answer is a nonresponse.

C7. Please describe your research capabilities.

Example C7-1

O'Keefe Guarantee is essentially self-sufficient in investment research. However, we have full access to research conducted by Wall Street and over 130 regional investment banking and brokerage firms.

Our Equity Research Department consists of 24 analysts and 3 assistant analysts who are supported by our internal Economics Department. Each analyst is broadly responsible for one industry area and specifically responsible for those companies within the industry. Analysts conduct fundamental research and periodically visit individual companies as they see fit. Internal research also includes contact with a wide network of political observers, foreign commentators, government experts, private economists, and market analysts (as well as the Wall Street and regional firms mentioned above).

Although our approach relies heavily on our computerized quantitative information, our analysts are particularly useful as a bankruptcy screen and in avoiding what are known as "torpedo" stocks (those companies with the capacity to deliver severe negative earnings surprises). This is analogous to credit analysis and "event risk" analysis on the fixed-income side (e.g., LBO downgrading of debt).

Much effort is concentrated on fostering communication of investment ideas throughout the firm, as well as within our Research Division. O'Keefe Guarantee has always supported the strongest in-house research effort and is essentially self-sufficient in investment research, utilizing a network of research analysts, assistant analysts, and a financial economist to generate 90% of all research.

The remaining 10% is obtained through an expansive group of political observers, foreign commentators, government experts, private economists, and market analysts. We have full access to Wall Street research and use it to correlate or challenge our in-house conclusions or provide background data. When utilized, outside research sources are subject to internal analysis before being incorporated into our investment process. Technical analysis is supplied by outside firms and is also used in a supplementary capacity. We maintain an extensive research library, which houses all external research deemed relevant by our professionals to investment policy. We make full use of internal distribution systems, on-line message screens, and research meetings to amplify ideas.

We develop our own economic viewpoint based on first-hand analysis of various monetary, government, international, and other economic factors. For fixed-income decisions, economic analysis is used as a primary tool in forecasting interest-rate changes.

Comments:

Applying good research to the investment process is crucial to some clients and irrelevant to others. In my personal view, firms wishing to remain on the cutting edge both in perception and in reality should have extensive research capabilities. I believe that the importance of manager emphasis on good research increasingly will predominate in the industry.

Four categories of research can be specified: (1) primary or internal research, (2) secondary or external research, (3) quantitative research, and (4) fundamental or company research.

O'Keefe generally does a good job in articulating the research efforts employed by the firm. Their discussion of internal research efforts, supplemented by external analysts, suggests that their market coverage is good. They also explain how the fundamental research helps them in their screens. Where O'Keefe falls down a bit is in explaining how their optimizer, the focal point of their investment process as discussed in example C2-4, is tested and refreshed through their research efforts.

C8. Please describe your trading practices.

Example C8-1

Our traders at Bierstadt, Inc., formally evaluate brokers we deal with semi-annually. Brokers are rated for cost, execution, and quality. They are also evaluated based upon their communication with us on carrying out orders, timeliness of trades, and their willingness to commit capital to us. In addition, we have participated in a trading costs study, which compares our trading activities to 26 other investment management firms. The results of both of these analyses help us to ensure effective, timely executions and control transaction costs.

Our primary concern is best execution. Brokers are rated based upon their willingness to commit capital, their responsiveness, information provided and timeliness of information, and price. Semiannually, our Head of Trading conducts a survey (written) to which all of our traders, analysts, and portfolio managers respond. The results of this survey in conjunction with our traders' ongoing, daily, documented experiences (based upon trade orders they undertake) form the basis for our monitoring of brokers.

Comments:

In the world where people fight for basis points, efficient trading methodologies can make a difference to the bottom line. Good monitoring of brokers as practiced by Bierstadt indicates a concern for detail and a concern for their clients' welfare.

C9. Please summarize your firm's unique characteristics versus your competition.

Example C9-1

Response by Remington & Associates

1. Our firm is a relative value investor, diversifying into several sectors of the economy.

2. We will not buy a company just because it is cheap, but only when a catalyst exists that will drive earnings higher in the immediate future.

3. We sell when a target price is achieved or the catalyst is lost or spent.

4. We have provided consistent, superior returns in all periods, whether in rising or falling markets.

5. Our investment team is diversified by age groups, giving a diversified perspective on all investment ideas.

Example C9-2

The unique attributes that distinguish Bierstadt's investment process are:

1. A top-down approach in a world of "stock pickers." Most small to mid-cap strategies focus upon stock picking. While our stock selection capabilities are the greatest source of our value-added (as verified through analysis by BARRA), our strategy begins with macro analysis aimed at identifying growth trends. This analysis enables us to focus upon the correct industries in order to screen stocks.

2. An exceptional research capability. While excellent research enhances and potentially adds value to a variety of investment strategies, it is particularly important for small to mid-cap managers. For small-mid-cap companies, there is information and insight to be gained through proprietary research. This is less true for large-cap, "blue-chip" companies.

3. Superior performance and a consistently applied investment process.

Example C9-3

We believe there are four principal characteristics that distinguish Sargent Trust from other firms.

1. Sargent Trust's investment services for retirement plans are based on proven investment disciplines that have superior long-term investment performance.

2. The sophistication of the risk-control process in our stock-selection process. We not only invest in the best available optimization software but we have made and continue to make proprietary supplements and enhancements to the software. This helps to maintain a flexible approach, which allows Sargent to best meet our clients' evolving needs.

3. Sargent Trust is committed to providing the resources necessary to support our investment professionals. Solid fundamental research augmented by sophisticated information and decision-making tools results in Sargent Trust's superior investment results. Our portfolio managers are spared no resource. Our clients benefit from major

in-house research facilities, sophisticated trading, and state-of-the-art systems.

4. Finally, we believe that the combined resources of Sargent Trust and the other affiliates in the Sargent Trust Group provide a unique blend of investment capability and knowledge. The key people at Sargent have proven records of success in the pension industry. This expertise produces extraordinary leverage for our clients.

Example C9-4

Five factors distinguish Cassat Investment Advisors from other investment mangers and our ability to add value to your mid-cap growth portfolio:

1. We have always adhered to our investment philosophy—accelerating and sustainable earnings growth in combination with relative price strength—for superior long-term returns.

2. We have successfully implemented our investment approach in the small- to mid-capitalization area for over 16 years.

3. Our research process combines the best of traditional early information networking with the discipline and controls of quantitative systems.

4. We have split our two main responsibilities—investments and client service—to ensure full attention to detail for our clients in both areas.

5. Currently, valuations in high-growth stocks are near the low end of their historical ranges, making this an extremely opportune time for our style of management.

Comments:

Without a doubt, this question provides the firm the opportunity to leap all the hurdles put forth by prospective clients. Yet, although the responses presented are among the best, I find that hardly anybody really maximizes this opportunity. Why should somebody hire or recommend hiring a firm if that firm itself cannot articulate well its own competitive advantages?

One would think that every quality organization should be able to sit down and ascertain its unique attributes, then list and describe those attributes to others. A list is more effective than straight prose. That list should, in aggregate, be able to go a long way in clearing the nine hurdles.

By now the reader of this book knows that the first hurdle to overcome is credibility. In the examples cited, only Sargent Trust and Cassat Investment Advisors really try to legitimize both their organization and its product in their responses. And neither one of them totally hits the mark. Sargent's attempt refers to their retirement plan services being "based on proven investment disciplines." Cassat promotes their "16 years of successfully implementing our investment approach." In order to effectively meet this hurdle, firms should articulate their unique history, role, and contributions to the investment industry.

Credentials are the second hurdle. Again, the responses are somewhat weak. Sargent again does the best in that they state that the "key people at Sargent have proven records of success in the pension industry." Well, that's fine, but what are the proven records of success? If I told the readers of this book that I am the foremost microbiologist in the world, they might be impressed. I suspect, however, that they would be less impressed if I failed to demonstrate any evidence of research, awards, or appropriate academic positions.

Again, the respondents fail to meet the third hurdle. Some response, if possible, that indicates the "recognition of others for outstanding returns and service" would be helpful.

Sargent and Cassat do better when it comes to addressing their responsiveness, the fourth hurdle. Sargent remembers its clients, using the word three times in the list. They "maintain a flexible approach which allows Sargent to best meet . . . clients' evolving needs," "clients benefit from major, in-house research facilities, sophisticated trading, and state-of-the-art systems," and "this expertise produces extraordinary leverage for . . . clients."

Cassat also lists responsiveness as a unique attribute: "We have split our two main responsibilities—investments and client service—to ensure full attention to detail for our clients in both areas."

On the fifth and last hurdle, nobody addresses the "importance of each individual client." They should.

All of the examples do a better job in addressing all or most of the strategic hurdles.

With respect to the sixth hurdle, investment philosophy, I like Bierstadt's approach of identifying themselves as top-down managers "in a world of 'stock pickers.'" They are appropriately characterizing their philosophy (and strategy) as different from that of the run-of-the-mill manager. Sargent Trust reinforces earlier responses by referring to "sophistication of the risk-control process" and the reasons for its sophistication as unique characteristics. Good job, Sargent.

Look at the first item on Cassat's list in example C10-4. Cassat effectively identifies the success of its investment philosophy and its consistency as unique characteristics.

The seventh hurdle, investment strategy, is nicely addressed in all of these responses. Remington reviews their strategy matter-of-factly and with conviction. I believe this approach works by announcing, "our unique characteristic is what we do." This approach would have worked better, however, if a list that tackled the soft hurdles was also presented.

Using the three items listed in example C10-2, Bierstadt reinforces the competitive advantages articulated earlier: unique approach, research, and stability (see examples C1-2 and C2-2). All these, if true, are characteristics grounded in the real world and are strengths.

Through its extensive discussion on research and resources, Sargent Trust effectively communicates the strengths of its investment strategy. Although they do not "prove" the merits of their statements, they articulate their position well.

The integrity of the investment process is the eighth hurdle. The clever manager will present attributes that provide confidence that the process will yield persistently positive results. Remington does the best job by reiterating the conviction of their process with superior results in rising or falling markets. Again, Bierstadt's approach of separating their philosophy from others and allowing them "to focus upon the correct industries" is a nice touch to overcome this hurdle.

One also perceives consistency from Sargent's "solid fundamental research augmented by sophisticated information and decision-making tools [resulting] in Sargent Trust's superior investment results."

Finally, Cassat invokes consistency by their research process, which combines "the best of traditional early information networking with the discipline and controls of quantitative systems." Unfortunately, Cassat shoots itself in the foot with their last statement about the "opportune time for our style of management." For long-term investors, this implies that there are times that are *not* opportune to invest in Cassat.

D. Performance and Performance Attribution

Performance as measured by returns is the bottom line. Even though some studies show that past performance is a poor proxy for future performance[2] most manager searches are affected by historical returns. Almost as important as the numbers themselves are the reasons for those numbers. Those reasons should be understood by the manager and explained qualitatively throughout the RFP.

They should also be explained quantitatively through the use of attribution analysis. Most people understand the limitations of common attribution analytical techniques; however, their use is invaluable in establishing some order of magnitude for the sources of value-added.

D1. For the subject product, describe causes for investment return deviation (both positive and negative) from the stated benchmark return by year and by account. Be detailed and specific.

Example D1-1

Although consultants occasionally attribute Remington's performance to good sector or industry bets, Remington & Associates process is bottom-up, so performance should be attributed to stock selection. Even if stock selection leads to good industry/sector results, it is not because of any top-down decision. No attribution study is available.

Example D1-2

Please see the exhibit on the following page [see Exhibit 1], which is a BARRA attribution of returns for Wyeth Company's value equity product

EXHIBIT 1. Wyeth Company

For Quarter Ended:	JUNE 1994	SEPT 1994	DEC 1994	MAR 1995	AVERAGE
RETURN FROM ACTIVE EXPOSURE TO:					
MARKET RISK	0.02	0.01	0.53	0.32	0.22
GROUP RISK	1.66	1.94	-1.55	3.90	1.49
INDUSTRY RISK	0.96	-0.38	-2.82	2.49	0.06
SPECIFIC STOCK RISK	1.49	2.99	1.06	0.99	1.63
OTHER	-0.02	0.27	-0.30	0.03	0.00
TOTAL ACTIVE RETURN	4.10	4.83	-3.10	7.73	3.39
TOTAL PORTFOLIO RETURN	3.87	10.21	5.22	5.20	6.13
ACTIVE RISK EXPOSURES:					
EQUITY BETA	1.16	1.19	1.18	1.15	1.17
GROUP EXPOSURES					
VARIABILITY IN MARKETS	0.63	0.87	0.86	0.73	0.77
SUCCESS	-0.40	-0.27	0.18	0.10	-0.10
SIZE	-1.58	-1.56	-1.14	-1.01	-1.32
TRADING ACTIVITY	0.15	0.26	0.31	0.33	0.26
GROWTH	0.29	0.35	0.06	-0.01	0.17
EARNINGS/PRICE RATIO	0.52	0.35	0.30	0.38	0.39
BOOK/PRICE RATIO	0.46	0.37	0.33	0.36	0.38
EARNINGS VARIABILITY	0.37	0.52	0.56	0.43	0.47
FINANCIAL LEVERAGE	0.37	0.35	0.37	0.27	0.34
FOREIGN INCOME	-0.45	0.35	0.44	-0.45	-0.42
LABOR INTENSITY	0.06	0.16	0.29	0.23	0.19
YIELD	-0.14	-0.26	-0.15	-0.01	-0.14
LOCAP	0.25	0.26	0.19	0.17	0.22

over the course of a year. Most of our return is attributable to our value style of management (group risk on the chart) and security selection (specific stock risk on the chart). Our value equity process has strict quantitative disciplines and uses strong, fundamental judgment to construct portfolios.

Example D1-3

The attribution analysis for all accounts managed by Gilbert Stuart Advisors in the subject product is shown [see Exhibit 2].

Example D1-4

Attribution analysis for the ten clients of George Bellows Associates in the subject product is shown on the following pages [see Exhibit 3].

EXHIBIT 2. Gilbert Stuart Advisors
Client A vs. Benchmark*

Year:	1994	1993	1992	1991
Total Difference[a]	-3.1	-3.4	+1.6	+3.4
TOTAL DIFFERENCE DUE TO:				
MARKET SELECTION	-0.4	+1.3	+1.2	-0.2
a. Mainstream Markets	-0.2	+1.3	+1.2	-0.2
b. Emerging Markets	-0.2	0.0	0.0	0.0
STOCK SELECTION	-5.1	-5.2	+1.7	+5.1
a. Large-Cap Exposure	-1.9	-3.8	+0.3	+4.2
b. Small-Cap Exposure	-3.2	-1.4	+1.4	+0.9
SECTOR SELECTION:				
Currency Exposure				
a. Unhedged	+0.6	+0.5	-0.5	-1.5
b. Hedged	+1.8	0.0	-0.8	0.0
Timing (cash)				
Timing (bonds)				
Other (specify)				

*MSCI Europe Index with dividends reinvested monthly.

[a]*Sum of difference factors* must total to "Total Difference" of the yearly return from the benchmark.

EXHIBIT 3. George Bellows Associates
Attribution Analysis

Client #1	1994	1993	Client #2	1994	1993
Fund	0.99	10.86	Fund	2.15	7.26
Benchmark	-4.25	14.59	Benchmark	-4.25	14.59
Variance	5.47	-3.26	Variance	6.68	-6.40
DIFFERENCE DUE TO:			*DIFFERENCE DUE TO:*		
Market Selection (Mainstream)	1.21	-0.12	Market Selection (Mainstream)	1.13	-0.01
Stock Selection (Large-Cap)	1.12	-2.40	Stock Selection (Large-Cap)	2.83	-5.99
Sector Selection	0.00	0.00	Sector Selection	0.00	0.00
Currency Exposure (Hedge effect)	2.58	-0.29	Currency Exposure (Hedge effect)	2.40	-0.10
Timing (cash)	0.03	0.73	Timing (cash)	0.00	0.17
Timing (liquidity)	0.30	-0.98	Timing (liquidity)	0.33	-0.79
Timing Total	0.33	-0.26	Timing Total	0.32	-0.62
Residual	0.14	-0.22	Residual	-0.14	0.30

Comments:

The response by Remington Associates is totally unacceptable. Companies will do well (or poorly) only if their product/service is in demand. Industry or sector returns represent the demand for that product/service. Companies that make more money than their competition do so because of better quality, distribution, or some other advantage. Unless we're talking about an industry with a limited number of players who control the market, industry or sector bets have meaning.

Even if Remington disagrees with this argument, the attribution must be provided if requested. In the response, Remington has the opportunity to express its viewpoint.

I noted how similar the investment strategies between Remington and Wyeth in the commentary for question C2. Whereas Remington begs the question of attribution, Wyeth provides detailed information in the form of BARRA statistics. This information reinforces Wyeth's strong orientation of providing quantitative discipline with fundamental judgment.

Although Wyeth's discussion of which group risk and which security selection risk factors were significant is weak, at least the factor values at several points in time are provided. Wyeth would have been given an A for the response rather than a B if they had explained the meaning of the factors and whether the biases would be persistent. If a normal portfolio had been established, providing that portfolio would have been useful.

Gilbert Stuart Advisors and George Bellows Associates provide the information as requested. Some qualitative interpretation of the numbers by each of the managers would have been helpful.

D2. Was the attribution analysis displayed above calculated internally or externally? If internal, please describe in detail the methodology used, the computer program source, and the securities database used. If external, please name your vendor.

Example D2-1

(Gilbert Stuart Advisors)

The attribution analysis displayed above was externally calculated by WM Company.

Example D2-2

(George Bellows Associates)

The attribution analysis was calculated internally.

The internal methodology used is laid out below.

All information is calculated in U.S. dollars, monthly, and then each month for the year chainlinked to arrive at an annual number.

- Calculate the monthly performance of the equities only, by each country within the portfolio. Use a time-weighted rate of return.

- Calculate the initial weighting of the fund for each month, by each country within the portfolio. This will sum to the percentage weighting of the fund in equities.

- Obtain from the relevant index supplier the initial weightings and the performance by country for the benchmark.

Total difference:

- The total fund return is chainlinked off from the total benchmark return.

Difference due to Stock Selection:

- Stock Selection is calculated by country by taking the difference between the performance of the fund in that country less the performance of the index in that country multiplied by the initial weighting of the fund in that country.

- Total Stock Selection for the month is calculated by chainlinking the stock selection for each country.

Difference due to Market Selection:

- Market Selection is calculated by country by taking the difference between the initial weighting of the fund in that country and the initial weighting of the index in that country, multiplied by the difference between the performance of the index in that country and the total benchmark return.

- Total Market Selection for the month is calculated by chainlinking the market selection for each country.

Currency Exposure (hedged):

- A weighted hedge return is calculated by weighting the hedge return for the month by the average weighting of the fund in hedges.

Timing (cash):

- A weighted cash return is calculated by weighting the cash return for the month by the average weighting of the fund in cash.

Timing (liquidity):

- The average weighting in cash for the month is multiplied by the negative of the total benchmark return for the month. This will calculate a return known as liquidity effect, which indicates the lost or gained opportunity of having held cash as opposed to equities.

Other (residual):

- This is the "balancing" item or unexplainable difference. By chain-linking each of the components as described above, and then taking the difference between this and the total difference, the resulting figure is the residual.

Comments:

Both Gilbert Stuart and George Bellows answered the question appropriately. Although not provided here, Gilbert Stuart included a letter of affirmation from WM as well as their attribution methodology. While using an external service to calculate attribution, George Bellows gives some assurance that the numbers are meaningful by detailing their procedures.

E. Client Service

E1. Who will be the client service officer? How often could he/she be available for client meetings? How often could the portfolio manager, chief investment officer, and/or firm president be available for client meetings?

Example E1-1

The main contact for your account would be Paul Gaugin, portfolio manager and CIO. A backup manager would also be assigned the account, for both management and meetings purposes. The average number of meetings Remington holds with its clients is about two per year, with one in our offices and one at the client's. We are prepared to meet quarterly if necessary, but often find quarterly meetings are not necessary. Any investment officer at Remington will be available at any reasonable time for contact with the client.

Comments:

I like Remington's response because they state that: (1) the CIO would be the main contact, (2) a backup officer would be assigned, (3) annual meetings at both the client's and advisor's offices is the standard practice, (4) more frequent meetings, but not a limitless number, would be provided, and (5) all investment officers would be available to clients. Clearly, Remington wants to balance accessibility to their clients with actual portfolio management.

E2. What unique educational or other client service capabilities can you offer a client?

Example E2-1

In addition to the monthly client report and a quarterly, which includes an investment overview and performance results on each of our products, we publish a quarterly newsletter for our clients.

Annually, Bierstadt sponsors a three-day seminar for its clients in Washington, D.C., which focuses upon economic, political, and social developments affecting and shaping the world, our lives, and the investment environment.

Our client service program is distinguished by our responsiveness and sound working relationships with our clients. The materials we share with our clients keep them well informed about our investment outlook and strategy and activities within their portfolios on an ongoing basis.

We meet with our clients quarterly or when they feel it is appropriate for us to do so based upon each of their needs. We maintain ongoing, informal contact via telephone as circumstances dictate. Our portfolio managers are available and accessible to our clients at all times.

Comments:

There are several schools of thought on managers providing educational programs. One is that advisors are hired to manage money and the "fluff" is expensive and distracts attention from that effort. The other school is that advisors have an implicit contract to help their clients to do their jobs better by imparting their expertise and knowledge.

Bierstadt takes the latter approach and communicates well. The combination of client reports, newsletters, broadly based informational seminars, and "responsive" client interactions certainly provides everything that clients would require. In order not to go overboard, they probably should state something like, "Bierstadt takes client service seriously and we believe we do it well. However, we hope that our clients appreciate that the bulk of our resources and attention must be focused on managing our clients' portfolios rather than on marketing activities."

CONCLUDING THOUGHT

In responding to questions, recognize that the reader is not particularly thrilled about wading through a lot of detail in the first round. Some readers are not thrilled at any time. My advice is to provide an executive summary with the key points that the advisor wishes the reader to remember. This will not only act as a quick synopsis for the first-time reader, but will act as a mnemonic thereafter.

Also, well-indexed appendices are a terrific invention. Detail displayed outside of the main text will allow the fastidious reviewer easy access without distracting from the main themes or bog down the more casual reviewer.

Remember, you want the reading to be as enjoyable and easy as possible (or at least not as painful as the competition).

Endnote

1. One more group should probably be identified: the manager whose recent performance has not been good. This manager may have lost clients or be in jeopardy of losing clients. Reestablishing a positive image for this manager may be even more of a challenge than for the emerging manager just getting started.

    It is crucial for managers with declining performance to emphasize the strengths that got them their business in the first place—experience, integrity of the firm, stability of the investment process. These managers must refer to later sections of the RFP, which will articulate why the investment decisions have not worked in the past, but will in the future. Alternatively, the manager can describe the modifications to the investment process that will turn around performance.

2. Ernest M. Ankrim, "Persistence in Performance," *Research Commentary*, Frank Russell Company, January 1992.

Chapter 7

FINAL PRESENTATIONS

In some cases, final presentations are perfunctory: the real hiring decision may already have been made and the final interviews exist to fulfill mandated procedures. In other cases, each of the three or four finalists in the beauty pageant have legitimate shots at being crowned the most beautiful. Like the event hosted by Bob Barker for so many years, there is little consolation for Miss Runner-Up in either case.

The final candidates themselves rarely know how they stand coming into the final stretch. They may or may not be aware of the identity of the competition. They may or may not know who among the decision makers are their supporters or their detractors, and the strengths of their convictions may be difficult to gauge. Usually, there is a time constraint placed on the presentation of anywhere from 15 minutes to 90 minutes. A multitude of questions may be asked during the presentation or after, or no questions asked at all. The floor must be yielded at all times when requested by those who deign.

PRESENTATION STRUCTURE

Most advisors get the general structure right. The outline should be some-thing like this:

I.   Introduction

    A. Introduce the Principals

    B. History of the Firm

    C. Investment Philosophy

II. Organizational Structure

III. Investment Strategy

IV. Investment Process

V.   Summary/Wrap-Up

    A. Tie Together Sections I-IV

    B. Detail Competitive Advantages

    C. Provide Blue-Chip Client List (if available)

    D. Describe Client Servicing

Although managers often prepare appropriate presentation outlines, imple-mentation can be very inconsistent. Usually, poor advisor presentations are a result of five factors:

1. Too little thought given to how the delivery might be perceived and thus coming across as either arrogant, condescending, or "too salesy."

2. An assumption that investment returns "speak for themselves," and a lack of understanding of the nine hurdles.

3. Becoming too bogged down on portfolio management issues to the exclusion of broader business issues.

4. Coming across as too rambling or too unfocused when responding to questions.

5. An inability to focus on concise themes and diverging from those themes.

PREPARATION RULES

Advisors who follow the seven prepatory rules will go a long way toward making a good impression.

1. The very first rule should be to revisit the make up of the board members and culture. Philosophy, level and type of expertise, individual and group personality types, etc., should be researched as much as possible. Presentations can be slanted accordingly.

2. The second rule in preparing the presentation is that the advisor must remember at all times that material should be geared toward overcoming the very same nine hurdles as all marketing efforts. The opportunity to present information and to develop theses obviously is limited. Thus, the emphasis must be focused differently. Quite likely, the board/committee members will rely on staff and consultants to understand the technical nuances of the manager's product.

To some degree, the length of time allocated to the interviews should be a signal as to what the emphasis of the presentation should be. As a general rule of thumb, interviews shorter than 30 minutes suggest that any substantive discussion of the investment philosophy, strategy, and process will be minimal. If the time allocated is between about 30 and 45 minutes, an opportunity to opine on the investment strategy probably will be available. Over 45 minutes, and the board/committee is probably prepared to discuss in some detail the investment process.

3. The third rule is that the message must parallel that conveyed in the written RFP. The careful reader will note discrepancies. This may seem simple enough, but this rule is all too often violated.

For example, I recall one manager who emphasized internal research capabilities in the RFP. Yet, once at the interviews, it became apparent that the investment process was more dependent upon outside input than primary research. Either the investment process was too ambiguous to provide a comfort level or the RFP writer was falsifying.

At any rate, this was enough of an issue to eliminate the manager from consideration.

4. The fourth rule is to use graphics and uncluttered charts to make points. If complex themes have not been absorbed by board/committee members when reading through the RFPs, they are unlikely to absorb them at the final presentations. Proving the manager's ingenuity and the sophistication of the investment program are not the goals of the presentation; the communication of clarity of purpose and the aura of success is.

5. The fifth rule is to "linearize" the presentation. Linearity means that statements should follow one another in logical sequence. One or two cause(s) will lead to one or two effect(s), with the latter becoming the cause for the next effect.

   Most people do not juggle multiple ideas and concepts in their heads at the same time. Advisors are usually very bright people who are intimately involved in their area of expertise. Therefore, jumping back and forth to many subjects is natural to their thought process. Generalizing that process to a formal presentation before an audience of nonexperts will result in utter confusion. Therefore, advisors should follow each point with a transition to the next point. Summations of where the presentation has been and where it is going will help.

   Remember that the tenets so embedded in the psyche of the advisors have to be communicated at a deliberate pace in order to be absorbed by the board/committee members, no matter how quick they are.

6. The sixth rule is to bring a minimum number of individuals to the presentation. Too many firm representatives are redundant at best and overwhelming at worst. My suggestion is that only those individuals representing three functional roles should be present: Client Service Officer, Senior/Founding Principal, and Chief Investment Officer. If the same individual functions in duplicate roles, less than three people is fine. Nobody else's presence is necessary.

   The person giving the introduction should be the person who will be the primary individual servicing the account. Unless the marketing person is a principal and intimately involved in the business and investment aspects of the firm, his/her presentation would be seen as a waste of time. If the marketing person will also be the client service officer, he or she must be an integrated component in the firm. If the marketing person is the only person who has had contact or *truly* does have personal relations with some of the decision makers, then he or she should come only to introduce the principals.

The Client Service Officer should present the introductory section. The organizational structure should be provided by a Senior Principal, while the Chief Investment Officer should review the investment strategy and process. The Client Service Officer should come back to tie things together, summarize, and wrap up.

7. The seventh rule is to rehearse in front of someone without a vested interest in the firm but knowledgeable in the industry, and therefore with the ability to be critically objective. The critic should be concerned about content, style of communication, and the pace of that communication. The critic should note when points are unclear, irrelevant to the main themes, or inconsistent, and remark if the speed of presentation is too slow or too fast.

THE PRESENTATION

By the time the actual oral presentation is made, the managers should be the most relaxed. The written material has spurred interest, the culture can be surmised, the presentation aids are well written, and the managers well rehearsed. At this point the managers have the opportunity to go out and be themselves.

Talking with people is much better than talking at them. Give your story, but be prepared to react when unexpected signals arise. If the audience looks disinterested, have some interesting anecdotes to tell that prove a point. If a sneer or raised eyebrow shows, stop and ask if there is a question or concern. Talk directly with people and appear interested in what you are saying.

I have a classic story that occurred at The Washington State Investment Board. In one search, staff was prepared to bring in six candidates with the idea that two would be hired. The same six emerged at the top of the list for all the individuals on the evaluation team. Unfortunately, at the last minute, one was forced to be eliminated because of major organizational upheaval. Rather than bring in only five, the team decided to go back to the pool and pick one more candidate ("Toulouse Lautrec Associates").

Both Mr. Toulouse, who was in his sixties, and Mr. Lautrec, who was in his fifties, came to the Committee. Mr. Toulouse was propped up by his cane, but had a liveliness and a presence that was captivating. Mr. Lautrec provided the serious pitch and Mr. Toulouse the seasoned commentary. After spending a perfunctory amount of time discussing the usual oratory requirements, they proceeded to illustrate their experience with personal tales of investment lore.

They captured the imagination of the Committee members. Their approach was brilliant. One of the Committee members wanted to give them the whole amount. When convinced that this was not such a good idea, the member insisted that the action resolution state the order of selection—with Toulouse Lautrec Associates as the clear number one.

As it so happens, and much to my surprise, Toulouse Lautrec has been one of the stars in The Washington State Investment Board stable of managers.

FEES

Thus far I have not discussed fees. Without question, the cost of investment management services can be a significant factor in the hiring process for many organizations. Also, without question, the subject of fees can be surprisingly irrelevant to other organizations.

Two characteristics of the money management hiring business dictate that the subject of fees traditionally does not come up until the time that the manager is selected. First, the exact product is usually not entirely understood until well along the evaluation process. It is hard to establish a price until one knows the attributes of the product. Once the attributes are ascertained, staff usually adopt the attitude of, "Why hassle about fees until we know for sure which of the finalists will be selected?"

Once selected, the second characterization dictates that the investment manager has significant pricing power. That is, once the anointed manager has differentiated himself by conveying unique characteristics, and those traits prove desirable, the manager faces an inelastic demand curve.

Having the client "on the hook," the price—and resulting gross margins—quite logically will be set high by the advisor. In order to not appear greedy, the advisor may wish to make some price "concession" at the end of the road. Of course, the greatest friend of the investment advisor has been the "most favored nations clause," which creates the illusion of having pricing flexibility being taken away from manager discretion.

The competition of the search, combined with pricing power, suggests that the investment management industry, in Schumpterian terms, could be thought of as being "monopolistically competitive."

To some degree, pricing power has declined recently. Pricing pressure has occurred as a result of increased plan sponsor sophistication and the demystification of portfolio management. In addition, studies have shown little correlation between manager fees and the ability to produce added value.[1] The use of performance-based fees, with all its operational problems, is an attempt by many plan sponsors to couple fees and performance.

A portion of RFP point scores are allocated to the cost of the money management service. However, except in the case of commodity-like products such as index funds, the points allocated are generally not enough to throw good managers out unless they are considerably out-of-whack. If managers are superior to the competition to make the final presentations, astute plan sponsors will apply pressure prior to those presentations to reduce fees.

The more control that the plan sponsor asserts in the implementation of portfolio strategies, the more likely that fees will be an issue. This is because plan sponsors know that the right allocation and exposures are more important determinants of return than the marginal value active managers can add. Consequently, they are always on the lookout for cheaper alternatives to active managers.

Along with some of my colleagues, I have on more than one occasion recommended to boards that they forego a manager because of fees when the second choice was a good alternative.

In one case, an RFP finalist had both higher portfolio turnover and higher fees versus the competition. Even though first choice of my Board in terms of meeting most of the hurdles, I pointed out that the fund would be 60 basis points behind the alternative right from the get-go because of these two factors. Even when confronted with our dilemma, candidate number one would not budge on fees at the final presentation. My board made the right decision to hire candidate number two.

My suggestion to money managers: keep fees near the middle of the pack, but be prepared to wheel and deal at the buzzer when attractive potential accounts press. No matter how good you think you are, you are not that much better than the next best competitor, both in reality and increasingly in the minds of many plan sponsors.

CONCLUDING THOUGHTS

The presentation should be considered an opportunity to "humanize" the firm, the people, and the investment program. Advisors should spend extensive preparation and *rehearsal* time in order to communicate consistent themes in a relaxed manner. To as great an extent as possible, the personalities of the decision makers individually and collectively should play a role in how to slant prepared materials and comments.

Obviously, there is no guarantee of success even when a perfect game plan has been crafted and implemented. Too often I hear the unsuccessful firm bellyache about the unfairness and prejudice of the decision-making process. These firms do not score any brownie points, and most people have long memories.

When not selected as an advisor, money management firms must maintain professionalism. Taking the high road is easy when one wins, difficult when one loses. Firms who lose and still maintain a positive attitude likely will have an opportunity to play again another day, in another arena. Situations change, organizations change, and people change.

The marketing effort should never stop.

Endnotes

1. Philip Halpern and Isabelle I. Fowler, "Investment Management Fees and Determinants of Pricing Structure in the Industry," *Journal of Portfolio Management*, Winter 1991, pp. 74–79.

Chapter 8

MAINTAINING POSITIVE RELATIONS BY MEETING CLIENT EXPECTATIONS

Without question, the best marketing strategy is to maintain the existing book of business. Readers now realize that hard work is necessary to win accounts. Once clients are won, it makes little sense to fritter them away because of poor client relations. The fact is that *marketing does not stop when the investment agreement is executed*. The nine hurdles must continue to be met, whether the goal is to maintain the client's existing business or to expand the services offered to the client.

Keeping the client happy means actively communicating why performance results occurred, what is going on in the firm, organizational changes, new areas of research, and so on. A happy client is more willing to ride the ups and downs of the market. Admittedly, the advisor may be given credit for general assistance in investment areas not directly related to the contractual mandate.

In other words, the investment advisor's behavior should be designed to make the client "want" the advisor to succeed. This statement may seem either obvious or absurd but, believe it or not, manager behavior often seems to suggest just the opposite.

I swear that one advisor at my current employer goes out of his way to make staff's life miserable. From the moment they were hired, they have been a pain in contract negotiations, investment guideline development, timely reporting, special projects, etc. I was once told when requesting special information that, "Our own needs do not require producing this information. Therefore, we see no need to honor your request." Needless to say, I was not pleased with this attitude.

There is only one absolute truth of the universe: money managers *must* service the needs of their client. Unless requests are blatantly outrageous, to refuse to do so or—even worse—to agree to a commitment and not to honor it is viewed very dismally indeed. The firm will be viewed as smug, unfocused, or out of control. None of these are good.

The intelligent plan sponsor should make very clear to its stable of money managers the expectations for success. If the client is unable to produce such a document and those expectations are not detailed in the Investment Agreement, the manager should consider providing a list of criteria.

Clearly, investment returns are the ultimate goal. At the very least, benchmarks should be clearly specified over a fixed time period. Objectives may require simply meeting the benchmarks, or may require exceeding the benchmarks by a certain number of basis points. In addition, return objectives might be risk-adjusted.

Appendix A of this book reproduces the external manager guidelines of The Washington State Investment Board, which is distributed and reviewed with each retained advisor. Not every sponsor is as precise in written form as Washington, but every manager has similar sets of requirements.

The Policy is designed to outline the five criteria for evaluating and monitoring manager overall performance: Return Performance, Style Integrity, Organization, Compliance, and Client Service.

RETURN PERFORMANCE

Not surprisingly, returns are the most carefully scrutinized evaluation criterion. Returns may be judged absolutely, relative to common benchmarks, or relative to custom benchmarks. Returns may also be compared against some risk-adjusted benchmark measure. The benchmarks may be defined as the best "passive alternative" or defined as some universe of comparable managers. There may be one benchmark or many, and the time frames for evaluation may be short or long.

The wise manager will request that the plan sponsor specify the benchmarks desired and sign off on that specification. The same advisor should determine as closely as possible how much tracking error is acceptable and how much time the advisor will have available to prove their ability to add value.

When the portfolio runs up against a bad quarter or two, it will be advantageous to have the ability to go back to the client and say, "What has happened is expected statistically, but we expect to still outperform the agreed-upon benchmark during the evaluation period." Believe me when I say that, if the parameters were not well understood initially, this argument is much less pervasive after the fact.

STYLE DEFINITION

The portfolio philosophy, strategy, and implementation process generally should not deviate from the time that the manager was hired. Modifications should be made only for clearly good reasons and, when made, clearly understood by the client.

Clients who closely monitor the portfolios will be on guard for changing portfolio characteristics. This sensitivity will be particularly heightened during periods of underperformance and periods of professional staff turnover.

Since most institutional investors select managers due to their expertise in certain niches, style drifts into other niches are absolutely forbidden.

ORGANIZATION

Advisors are hired only when they satisfactorily meet hurdles of credibility and credentials. Should the firm's ownership structure change or personnel be hired or dismissed, the chemistry is altered. It may be that the changes are positive, and certainly without denying staff losses they should be couched as such, but uncertainty will undoubtedly increase.

How the manager handles inevitable evolution in the firm's structure says a lot about the principals' business acumen. It is much easier to manage a business when times are good, the external environment is stable, and nobody grows old, dies, or finds better opportunities. However, things do change and the advisor must be prepared to minimize any real or perceived slight to the client.

Along these same lines, changes in the number of accounts and assets under management should be explained to the clients. Astute plan sponsors, who are ever increasing in number, will want to know how the business is doing along with portfolio returns.

The honest, diligent advisor will keep clients abreast of what's going on.

COMPLIANCE

Compliance comprises two components: meeting legal and regulatory statutes and meeting client-specific requirements. It goes without saying that advisors had better meet government mandates (e.g., antitrust, securities law, registration) or they will be censored or worse. Most advisors most of the time do not run afoul of these mandates.

Compliance with client-specific requirements includes such things as investment guidelines, reporting requirements, and proxy voting guidelines. These requirements generally are clearly spelled out in the investment management agreements. Most violations occur with respect to the investment guidelines.

Compliance seems to be an area over which managers have absolute control, yet one where performance varies extensively. Some managers are very fastidious about ensuring that investments are undertaken strictly in accordance with clients' investment guidelines. Many of these have spent significant sums of the firm's capital in developing tracking systems to alert the portfolio manager to trades that could potentially violate the guidelines.

Other managers have the attitude, "Damn the guidelines," and invest the same no matter what the guidelines say. The most common violations include too much cash (e.g., often clients set a ceiling of 5% of assets). Others include buying fixed-income securities with too long a maturity, creating a fixed-income portfolio with too long a duration, being over-hedged, and having too much exposure to one country.

Finally, some advisors push the guidelines to the limit even though technically they are not in violation. One egregious example comes to mind. One of my managers was allowed to use derivatives to adjust duration in a fixed-income portfolio indexed to the Lehman Government/Corporate benchmark. I discovered that this advisor had purchased several asset-backed securities, which are neither government securities nor corporate securities. By some definitions, these securities might be considered derivatives. Yet, even if technically true, it should have been quite obvious that the inclusion of these securities was not intended for this portfolio.

To add insult to injury, the securities were private placements and very illiquid! Although the investment guidelines (which I inherited, by the way) did not preclude private placements, again it is obvious that they should not have been included in the investment mandate. Do you think this manager earned goodwill with me? Not Likely!!!

Quite honestly, the discrepancy in the compliance track records of managers suggests to me that the majority of clients do not monitor their investments closely. If they did, managers who do not develop a good system of ensuring compliance would not be able to remain in business for very long. I have to wonder in this case why clients even bother to establish guidelines other than for the perfunctory exercise of satisfying fiduciary requirements.

My advice to the manager is not to count on the client ignoring compliance issues.

CLIENT SERVICE

Client service really incorporates all aspects of managing the client's portfolio. A formal schedule of communications to discuss these aspects should be initiated by the manager, if not by the client. Two times a year is probably adequate, unless major market- or firm-specific events dictate more frequent visits.

Where the exceptional managers separate themselves from the merely adequate is in their ability to perform special requests. Many plan sponsors will use their money managers in consulting roles. Some argue that professionals who are in the markets every day can bring insight into a number of strategic issues that supplements advice offered by the traditional consultants. In this vein, managers should be prepared to offer portfolio expertise and to perform research as requested.

The client service efforts should address the "new paradigm" trend discussed in Chapter 9.

MANAGER TERMINATION

Unfortunately, managers sometimes do get fired. This subject is not pleasant to think about, but important to discuss nonetheless.

Without exception, hurt and dismay are the natural feelings for the manager who is terminated. Although it is sometimes hard for plan sponsors to believe, money managers also are human beings.

If the client and the advisor are communicating, termination should never be a surprise. In the case of strategic change or corporate governance changes, there may be little the manager can do to save the account. Advisors feeling the ill effects of these changes can only lament that life is not always fair.

Terminations in the case of failing client expectations are another matter. Although clients are never pure in their communication efforts, managers usually should know what is expected in terms of performance and other criteria. If managers are not performing, the relationship must end.

Whatever the reason for termination, professionalism must be maintained even when hurt and dismay are overwhelming. One never knows when the individual decision makers will reenter the advisor's life at some point in the future. A sour grapes attitude will never help and, quite possibly, will come back to haunt some day.

One time I inherited a manager that I had previously fired for underperformance when working for another organization. I was impressed at the high road they had taken during my first experience and their assistance in making the transition to their successor. When I encountered them the second time, I was more than willing to give them the benefit of any doubt.

Even though I had to fire them years earlier, they earned my respect and goodwill. Today, we are all good friends.

It has been remarked that the only absolute in the universe is that there are no absolutes. The world changes and one never knows who we will run into again and in what circumstances. Best to act professionally and cordially all the time, to everyone.

CONCLUDING THOUGHTS

Money management is a service industry. Money managers do not produce toasters and minivans. If the client is happy with the service, the client will continue paying the fees that the manager charges. If unhappy, there are plenty of other firms eager to provide the service to that client.

I urge both advisors and plan sponsors to read The Washington State Investment Board's monitoring policy included as Appendix A. My staff (particularly Nancy Calkins) has articulated on paper a very comprehensive rulebook that most plan sponsors use to play.

Chapter 9

CURRENT EMERGING TRENDS IN THE MARKETPLACE

A s elaborated upon throughout this book, change is endemic to the investment management industry. Without a doubt, all plan sponsors will feel the pressure of the emerging trends in the marketplace. With the onslaught of articles, speeches, conferences, and peer pressure, no plan sponsor has the ability to ignore these trends. Some plan sponsors will recognize the associated opportunities, leading to new business for managers.

Discriminating between trends that are real and sustainable and current fads is not a trivial challenge. For example, I am reminded of the publicity over the past several years regarding Economically Targeted Investments (ETIs). ETIs are fascinating, not because of what they represent, but because discussions seem to have taken on a life of their own. In reality, there is scant evidence that ETIs have taken on a significant role in defined benefit plans. The endless calls that I receive from publicity-seeking individuals requesting The Washington State Investment Board's "position" does not change that fact.

Yet, clearly, several recent trends emerging in the pension plan world are affecting the way in which investment portfolios will be structured.

Greenwich Associates is perhaps the foremost institution for research and analysis of changes in this marketplace. Their information is gathered first-hand through extensive interviews with hundreds of large corporations, public funds, endowments, and foundations. In the 1994 report, Greenwich identifies significant patterns.[1]

Keeping an eye on the market, and reacting appropriately, will allow the wise investment advisors to develop the successful investment products of the future. The following list of trends are taken largely from Greenwich Associates' fine work.

THE INCREASING ROLE OF DEFINED CONTRIBUTION PLANS

The shift from defined benefit plans toward defined contribution plans is one major example of employer response to a changing world. In the age of rapidly evolving technology, industry restructurings, and rationalizations, most corporations no longer can afford to carry an uncertain pension liability. In addition, a mobile workforce often prefers transferable 401(k) benefits to pensions. Greenwich reports that:

> Fully 97% of all large U.S. companies, in fact, now use some kind of defined contribution plan, and our research consistently demonstrates that pension plans are emphasizing and reemphasizing defined contribution development. When asked about the most important initiatives they expect to take in the next year or two, consultant Michael Kustra notes that a strikingly high proportion of pension officials speak of initiating additional defined contribution plans, of developing their existing plans in one important way or another, and of focusing on defined contribution rather than defined benefit in the future.[2]

Greenwich also reports that 37% of benefit assets were represented by defined contribution assets as compared to 30% only four years before. Pension officials predict that the percentage will go up to 60% in ten years.

In addition to reasons cited earlier, the recent trend toward defined contribution plans by companies is an attempt to reduce fiduciary liability by giving participants individual discretion over decisions and thereby relieving the sponsoring institution of some of its responsibility. As Chris McNickle from Greenwich asserts, "Defined benefit plans create a liability that corporations cannot accurately assess in advance, but for which they are legally responsible, and defined contribution plans do not."[3]

Although less common on the public side, the same forces have begun to influence some states, including my home state of Washington, to consider moving towards a DC plan.

Organizations with a paternalistic culture may consider DCs' self-direction features a drawback rather than a virtue. Not only does the corporation lose the ability to protect the employee as its agent, but the employer loses the control of the retirement carrot. Future incentives in the nature of cash flow during retirement years if the employee sticks around are no longer present. Thus, the concept of "loyalty" to the employing organization is undermined. Of course, recent rationalizations, takeovers, and cutbacks make the notion of paternalistic employers anachronistic.

Implication for Money Managers

The kinds of products that will appeal to self-directed participants have different characteristics from those that appeal to corporate defined benefit sponsors. Requirements for managing money in DC plans may differ from DB plans in two key areas. First, communications to nonprofessionals are even more important. Sponsors fight an uphill battle to communicate the advantages of equity-like strategies, especially to younger participants. Index funds are easily explained and, hence, are popular alternatives for sponsoring organizations to offer. Active managers should be cognizant of this disadvantage and should avoid at all costs obtuse communications. Products that are difficult to understand will be difficult to sell both to sponsors and to participants.

Second, the asset mix for defined contribution plans is quite different than for the traditional defined benefit plan. Greenwich research makes this point clearly:

> Between domestic and international stocks and equity real estate, more than 60% of corporate defined *benefit* assets are invested in equities of one kind or another; between domestic and international bonds and guaranteed investment con-

tracts, just over 30% are in long-term fixed-income. In contrast, between cash, bonds, and GICs, defined *contribution* plans now have 45% of their assets in fixed-income investments, and they put just over 50% in equities—including no less than 31% in *company* stock.[4]

The disenchantment by plan sponsors with GICs clearly represents a huge opportunity for investment advisors. Until 1993, many staff members had received very lukewarm responses from their committees when warning them of the dangers of guaranteed investment contracts. It took the well-publicized woes of Mutual Benefit and Executive Life—two major issuers of GICs—to get some people's attention. It is interesting how few money management firms anticipated the problems of GICs by developing competing products. Even today, stable fixed-income alternatives to the guaranteed products have not been exploited to a great extent by money managers.

Finally, risk control within each investment option is even more paramount than for DB plans. Participants who feel that they were taken advantage of because they did not understand the risks will go after the sponsoring organizations (e.g., Mutual Benefit and ARCO). In these circumstances, the corporation negates the major advantage of risk transference inherent in participant-directed plans. Products that closely track well-known benchmarks and still add value should be attractive to defined contribution programs.

INCREASED OVERSEAS INVESTMENTS BY INSTITUTIONS

The significance of cross-border investments has been discussed extensively for both investor portfolios specifically and the world's economies in general. According to the analysis by Michael J. Howell and Angela Cozzini from Baring Securities, net equity overseas investments by U.S. investors increased from about $10 billion in 1990 to an estimated $66 billion in 1993. They state that something like one stock trade in four around the world involves a foreign share or a foreign investor as a counterparty.[5]

Greenwich reports several findings that all indicate the same trends. The percentage of funds investing overseas increased from 50% in 1992 to 57% in 1993. Average assets by funds in their universe grew from an average of

7% to 8% in that same single-year period, while plan officials anticipate overseas investments will represent 12% by 1996.

Combined with this movement, and not totally independent, is the improvement in overseas custodial and trading practices. In order to attract capital against competing uses as markets develop, local companies and exchanges will have to meet rigorous accounting and reporting standards.

Implication for Money Managers

Obviously, money managers who already provide the organization and products geared toward overseas investments have been and will continue to jump up and down and clap their hands in excitement. In 1993, Greenwich reports that the number of new international managers hired outnumbered terminations by six to one!

Areas to focus on include public funds, the great sources of capital who are taking a major leap forward in international investing, and also defined contribution plans that have had limited exposure (only 1% of DC assets are invested abroad according to Greenwich Associates).

Those firms who were not early entrants to overseas investing have attempted to transfer their domestic experience to international markets. Unfortunately for the later entrants, the trend of institutions moving assets abroad has not gone unnoticed. Thus, the competition to become significant players in these markets will be tougher.

Firms that will be successful in attracting assets may do so by paralleling their unique domestic investment philosophy/strategy/process to the foreign arena. Also, these firms may identify a niche (e.g., regional focus, small-cap stocks, emerging stocks) and establish an expertise that heretofore has not been exploited. If that niche has a recognized, parallel counterpart in the domestic markets, that identification and exploitation will obviously be made easier. Improved reporting data and available statistics obviously will work to the benefit of money managers trying to become niche players.

FOCUS ON EFFICIENCY/RATIONALIZATION OF MANAGER STRUCTURE

Greenwich Associates notes that 30% of all funds terminate one or more of their investment managers annually. This turnover, suggests their consultants, is as often the result of a change in fund policy as it is due to poor manager performance. They attribute this phenomenon to the emergence of the "new paradigm" of investment management. According to Charles D. Ellis, Managing Partner of Greenwich Associates:

> The new paradigm firm offers pension plans a new way to get the majority of their assets managed under a single roof—and to get them managed cohesively according to strategic goals and objectives. It is totally different from the "specialist" models that have dominated pension fund investment management for the past two decades and also totally different from the old "balanced" management model—because it is based on a much deeper client-manager relationship.[6]

Greenwich has articulated well the trend that has been occurring for many plans. They intimate that the key reason for development of the paradigm and the concomitant "strategic relationship" is the desire of the plan sponsor to develop an intimacy with world-class advisors. That intimacy takes the form of a deep understanding of the fund's needs and objectives and can only occur by the fund providing significant business to the advisor. In fact, under the new paradigm, Greenwich suggests that advisors not only react to client goals, but assist in their development.

There is no question that a multiple manager structure is cumbersome to oversee and expensive because of excess trading, monitoring, and management fees. What Greenwich fails to explore is the reason that single "trust" accounts were discarded: (1) manager risk increased because of overdependence on a limited number of outside firms, (2) mediocre overall performance resulted because broad-based firms did not create the culture to be outstanding in all important market niches, and (3) insufficient control was exercised by the client.

I do not believe that the "new paradigm" totally addresses these three risks. First, should the firm have organizational upheaval, a larger portion of the portfolio is exposed under this model.

Second, there is limited evidence suggesting that the best firm in U.S. equity markets is also the best in international equities or international bonds. Many of the best money managers are individualistic and entrepreneurial, which makes them resistant to working in large organizations.

Finally, the new paradigm transfers a greater proportion of decisions to downstream agents. Hence, the danger of increased conflicts of interest arises. For example, money mangers may wish to transfer a portion of assets from U.S. equities to emerging markets, not because it is in the greater interest of their client, but because they want to build up a track record in that area.

I would like to broaden the trend identified by Greenwich to the desire for greater control and efficiency. Plan sponsors can achieve this goal in one of *two* ways: they could take the form of the "new paradigm" or they could reduce external manager discretion by taking more active/centralized decision making in-house. These are not necessarily inconsistent, but they are not identical.

Both approaches would account for the reduction in the number of advisors as identified by Greenwich. Plan sponsors wishing to take greater control would strive to achieve portfolio diversification through active market segment and factor exposure management, rather than through hiring a proliferation of "styles" associated with multiple managers. One typical model employs an "index-like" portfolio managed by a single manager combined with a limited number of specialized managers who have defined, nonduplicative niches.

I believe that Greenwich has actually identified a result of a broader trend, not the trend itself. The trend is the desire on the part of many plans to manage more efficiently.

Implication for Money Managers

Whatever the reason for the rationalization of managers, implications are clear. Under the new paradigm scenario, the manager must develop a multiple product line. They need not be the best in everything, but the best in one thing and pretty good in many areas. The need to demonstrate skill in policy development, active asset allocation, and other macro kinds of skills are necessary. Essentially, under the new paradigm, the money manager must be able to combine the talents of the traditional consultant with those of the traditional money manager.

Managers who seek out business from plan sponsors employing the new paradigm must emphasize the breadth of the organization and the importance of the entire team seeing the whole picture. Consistency of philosophy and decision making across asset classes would be paramount. Initiative and individual insight must, in a sense, be subservient to this consistency. The culture of the new paradigm firms must be a corporate culture because the organizational resources necessary to marshal the broad-based mandate are extensive.

Since the new paradigm firms manage significant percentages of their clients' assets, the danger of making a hiring mistake is even more significant. It is unlikely that firms that already do not have long track records and stellar reputations would be able to compete.

Under the active/centralized form of control, the requirements of the plan sponsor may be different. Managers who have distinct and superior products in limited market segments or niches should be able to keep and win business. However, it is crucial that the specialty or boutique managers keep in mind the kind of portfolio structure employed by the plan sponsor and the appropriate role for their product.

Uniqueness is key for the specialist firm, whereas, for the new paradigm firm, uniqueness may be actually a handicap. This is because the unique characteristics that might work in one asset class (e.g., macro, quantitative management in the U.S. markets) may not work in other asset classes (e.g., micro, fundamental management in the emerging markets). The personalities of the portfolio managers and kinds of resources required would have to be different. Could such an organization maintain consistency and control of its culture? I think not.

Instead of the uniqueness of the boutique manager, the new paradigm manager would need to adhere to established principles and emphasize their strengths of implementation.

INCREASED EMPHASIS ON PRIVATE MARKET INVESTMENTS

Plan sponsors are increasingly interested in private market investments or alternative investments. For example, Private Equity Analyst reports that $19.4 billion in new private equity commitments were made in 1994, a 51% increase from the year earlier and a 30% compounded annual increase from 1990.[7] According to the National Venture Capital Association 1993, about half of venture capital commitments come from pension plans.

The expectation of higher returns is the attraction of investing in private market instruments. Of course, economic risk, liquidity risk, and corporate governance risk are concomitantly greater. I generally like to classify these into three broad categories: operating companies (e.g., all stages of venture capital, buyouts, distressed companies) asset-driven investments (e.g., oil and gas, timber, agriculture), and special situations (e.g., managed futures, arbitrage, long-short, subordinated private commercial mortgages).[8]

The difference between private investments and public market investments are many. Listed below are a few.

1. Public market investments are generally widely followed and continually priced in a well-established exchange or over-the-counter network. Private market investments have none of these characteristics.

2. Investors in private markets are not just passive investors, but actively involved in value creation (i.e., either directly or through their general partners). For example, companies have some franchise value in terms of technology, proprietary production systems, or superior distribution systems. Value is created by assisting the company in moving from one life cycle stage to another.

   The provision of capital is just one form of assistance. "Sweat equity" or "intellectual equity" is the value added to the enterprises through hard work and insight.

3. In many private operating company investments and to a limited extent in the other categories, investors are "price-makers," not just "price-takers." That is, barriers to entry combined with the franchise value allow companies to realize abnormal profits. This is in contrast

to investing in the public markets where companies are priced "efficiently."

4. Since valuation creation is a long-term proposition, the commitment is much longer. An equity or bond manager can be fired in a matter of days; the private market fund manager has a fixed-term, renewable contract.

Market value cannot be accurately determined until the investments have been sold. Interim evaluation of the fund managers' performance during the contract period is not very meaningful.

5. In investing in private market opportunities, the franchise value reflects the abilities of people—the general partners (GPs). In other words, institutional investors are buying the GPs' deal flow, due diligence process, and ability to realize value from their sweat equity and intellectual equity. In effect, the institutional investor's net equity is largely made up of "goodwill."

6. Except for asset-driven investments, the true investment returns are highly dependent upon the skill of the general partners. This dependency is reflected in the fact that "managing to benchmarks or to the passive alternative" is not meaningful. Benchmarks that do exist are tied toward some universe of partnerships rather than to a universe of securities.

7. Since returns are highly dependent on the skill of GPs, the investor must pay high management fees and carried interest (i.e., performance-based fees). These costs are much greater than investing in the public markets through advisors—in fact, *very* much greater. As opposed to the relatively little negotiation characteristic of public markets, the terms and conditions of private market transactions are thoroughly negotiated.

8. For all the business reasons, the governance structure outlined in investment management agreements or subscription agreements tends to be very complicated. The terms of compensation outlined in the agreements are more complicated in addition to being higher.

As limited partners, institutional investors have very little control over the partnership investments once that investment is made.

Private investing must seem very strange to those living in the world of public markets. Why would institutional investors entrust significant amounts of capital to such a beast?

Well, let's identify several reasons underlying the move toward private market investments. First, opportunities to add value in the public markets are viewed as limited. Fewer and fewer institutional investors that I know are excited by U.S. publicly traded stocks and bonds. With so much widely disseminated information and armies of bright analysts poring over public information, the likelihood of generating excess returns in the public markets is minimal. Strategies that may look good often entail some nonsystematic bet (e.g., leverage, industry bets, sector bets, duration bets, prepayment risk) and may succeed only at the margin.

I cannot remember having any peer tell me, "Boy, I discovered this terrific large-cap growth manager." This is not to say that investors do not try to find that outstanding large-cap growth manager, but the search is rarely satisfying.

The second reason for identifying private market investments as an emerging trend is the ability of the managers to actually do something in the real world, not just in the financial world. This is true not only for the individual investments in the portfolio, but the portfolio strategy.

In contrast, institutional investors are spending increasing percentages of their time searching for partnerships that add value. And, in many instances, they will develop ideas and search for players to implement those strategies. General Motors, for example, spent years trying to develop a means to participate in the burgeoning securitization market of commercial mortgage-backed securities. Working with Blackrock (a major fixed-income manager) and the Bass Brothers organization (a major real estate player), GM was able to devise an extremely innovative method of participation. To my employer's good fortune, The Washington State Investment Board was able to join GM, GE, and others as partners in this investment. Blackrock is a good example of how an investor can exploit a changing economy and participate in gains through the securitization of new types of instruments.

Third, there is some evidence that the relatively young private markets for institutional investors add diversification to the overall portfolio. For example, venture capital funds committed in the 1970s did very well, while the U.S. stock market returns were poor for much of that period. The reverse occurred in the 1980s:.many private market partnership returns were poor, while public market returns were terrific. A growing number of people now believe that private capital opportunities are on the uptick.

Fourth, even during the doldrums of the 1980s, some partnerships continued to do exceptionally well. Unlike advisors in the public market who operate on similar playing fields, success has a tendency to feed on itself in private markets. This is because the best operators, brokers, and investors will want to continue to do business with the best general partners. Thus, once you get with a winner, the chance of future success is greater.

Implications for Money Managers

Some traditional money management firms have extended their product lines into the private market area (e.g., Brinson Partners, Chancellor). I know of many other firms thinking of doing the same thing.

There is some pressure by major institutional investors to reduce the costs of doing business in this area. One area that is sure to come under scrutiny is the profits paid to the general partners. However, most incentives for success undoubtedly will be maintained. This is a highly profitable business.

Once a fund is raised with a good client base, efforts can be devoted to running the portfolio and not raising capital. If the fund is successful, a new fund can be raised toward the end of the life of the initial fund. Most likely, existing clients will reinvest and will naturally attract other, like-minded investors. Unlike money management, fund sizes are fixed and asset size becomes the problem not for the advisor but for the investor: how not to be closed out of successful partnerships.

Private equity advisors with expertise in international markets may be able to exploit two of the four trends discussed in this chapter. However, anecdotally, there seem to be many more players trying to capture these two trends than are really qualified.

The trend toward defined contribution plans may have a long-term negative impact on private equity investing. This is because the liquidity required in participant-directed plans makes private investing more difficult.

CONCLUDING THOUGHTS

One of my previous bosses once told me that there are two choices in life: move ahead or fall behind. The same implication for money managers is clear: change with the times or begin planning for your retirement.

No matter how many basis points the advisor earns today, forgetting the fundamental planning, marketing, and communication skills stressed in this book will significantly reduce chances for future success.

Endnotes

1. "Seismic Shift in Pension Planning," *Greenwich Report,* Greenwich Associates, 1994.

2. *Ibid.*, p. 2.

3. *Ibid.*, p. 2.

4. *Ibid.*, p. 3.

5. Michael J. Howell and Angela Cozzini, "Cross-Border Equity Flows: Hot or Cold?" *The GT Guide to World Equity Markets 1994-1995,* Euromoney Publications Plc, 1994, pp. 12-23.

6. "Seismic Shift in Pension Planning," *Greenwich Report,* Greenwich Associates, 1994, p. 9.

7. "Fund Raising Soared to Record in 1994, Reaching $19.4 Billion," *The Private Equity Analyst*, January 1995.

8. Technically, some alternative investment opportunities may employ the use of publicly traded securities. However, all strategies in this category share many of the same types of return-risk characteristics, liquidity constraints, and other features.

   The reader may note that I have excluded real estate from this discussion. With the possible exception of distressed real estate, leveraged real estate, or development property, high expected returns generally are not the compelling reason why plan sponsors invest in this asset class. Anyway, I do not consider some renewed interest in real estate as an emerging trend, but rather another phase in the long cycle of institutional investment.

Chapter 10

CONCLUSION

I was fortunate recently to spend time with Richard Rainwater at an intimate seminar sponsored by Elkind Economics. His many successes have included a profitable career with the Bass Brothers and entrepreneurial start-ups of Columbia, and Crescent REIT. His manner is impressive in its forthrightness, animation, and clarity.

Mr. Rainwater discussed two competitive disadvantages that tax-exempt institutions must overcome when playing the investing game. First, the distractions characteristic of large organizations impede the ability to make quick and focused decisions. Mr. Rainwater does not have oversight committees, or numerous memos to write. Nor does he have a large organization to manage. Instead, he and his limited staff spend their time on only one thing: how to make money.

Second, the size of the asset base and close scrutiny prevents the opportunity to focus on a limited number of themes or investments. Mr. Rainwater does not dispute the idea of diversification but, when carried to the extreme, it can result in only one thing: mediocre returns.

For example, at the time of his comments in the fall of 1994, Mr. Rainwater was not convinced that overall real estate investments would be attractive in the near term. He believed that institutions who reentered the market by "diversifying" simply would not do well. Yet, Mr. Rainwater recently had made significant real estate purchases. But, importantly, these purchases were made in selected areas in about 10 cities. Mr. Rainwater was able to differentiate between the characteristics of the overall market and the unusually attractive nature of each specific investment.

I have thought a lot about Richard Rainwater's comments. I suspect that in the long run, Mr. Rainwater's portfolio will outperform any investment program put together by me or other plan sponsors. This is not just because Mr. Rainwater is incredibly astute, which he is. My suspicion is based on the fact that his insights about the constraints of running money for tax-exempt institutions are exactly on target.

Yet, when analyzing investment opportunities, the same types of hurdles must be overcome by any potential partner with whom Mr. Rainwater would consider investing. For the tax-exempt institutional investor, the fiduciary roles defined by regulation and the resulting corporate governance structures impede the incentives and flexibility to make optimum economic decisions at all times. Board and staff members, individually and collectively, will not make the same decisions that direct owners of capital would make with the same knowledge and expertise.

This is not to say that all is woe. Most institutional investors are diligent within their own governance and cultural parameters. Money managers who wish to be retained as agents simply must recognize those parameters if they want any chance to influence decisions.

Advisors should not assume that what is working in today's marketplace will work in tomorrow's marketplace. They should not guess what clients want, they should ask. "Clients" are made up of groups of individuals, with individual needs, goals, and career objectives.

Advisors who believe that their business is exempt from sound business planning and marketing principles are unlikely to survive in a competitive, sophisticated marketplace.

Most of what is discussed in this book is common sense to most institutional money managers. Yet, that common sense so often gets lost in the pressures and fast pace of the moment. If advisors choose to plan a little more and react a little less after reading these chapters, then I will feel that I have achieved my mission.

BIBLIOGRAPHY

Keith Ambachtsheer, "Is Pension Fund Management Really Monkey Business?" *The Ambachtsheer Letter*, Toronto Canada, November 22, 1993.

Ernest M. Ankrim, "Persistence in Performance," *Research Commentary*, Frank Russell Company, January 1992.

"The Coming Investor Revolt," *Fortune*, October 31, 1994, pp. 66–76.

"External Manager (Public Securities) Monitoring," *The Washington State Investment Board*.

"Fund Raising Soared to Record in 1994, Reaching $19.4 Billion," *The Private Equity Analyst*, January 1995.

"Gatekeepers Keep Big Role in Selection," *Global Finance*, Global Finance Joint Venture, New York, January 1995, pp. 25-26.

Philip Halpern and Isabelle I. Fowler, "Investment Management Fees and Determinants of Pricing Structure in the Industry," *Journal of Portfolio Management*, Winter 1991, pp. 74–79.

Philip Halpern, "ERISA and the Agency Problem: The Impact on Corporate Pension Plan Performance," *The Journal of Investing*, Fall 1993, pp. 7–16.

Douglas K. Harman, *How to Start Your Own Money Management Business* (Burr Ridge, IL: Richard D. Irwin, Inc. 1994).

Michael J. Howell and Angela Cozzini, "Cross-Border Equity Flows: Hot or Cold?" *The GT Guide to World Equity Markets 1994-1995*, Euromoney Publications Plc, 1994, pp. 12–23.

Michael C. Jensen, "Eclipse of the Public Corporation," *Harvard Business Review*, September-October 1989.

Carl Jung, *Psychological Types* (New York: Harcourt Brace, 1923).

David Keirsey and Marilyn Bates, *Please Understand Me: Character & Temperament Types* (Del Mar, CA: Prometheus Nemesis Book Company, 1984).

Josef Lakonishok, Andrei Shleifer, and Robert Vishny, "The Structure and Performance of the Money Management Industry," *Brookings Papers on Economic Activity*, 1992, pp. 339–91.

Marketing and Merchandising, Volume 5 in the series Modern Business, The Alexander Hamilton Institute, New York, 1918.

William M. O'Barr and John M. Conley, "Managing Relationships: The Culture of Institutional Investing," *Financial Analysts Journal*, September–October 1992, pp. 21–27.

Russell K. Mason, "Market or Go Out of Business," *Effron Report*, Year End 1993.

Money Management Letter, October 24, 1994, vol. XIX, no. 22, p. 1.

"Seismic Shift in Pension Planning," *Greenwich Reports*, Greenwich Associates, 1994.

EXTERNAL MANAGER MONITORING POLICY

INVESTMENT POLICY

POLICY NUMBER: 3.30.100

TITLE: External Manager
     (Public Securities) Monitoring

EFFECTIVE DATE: 10/27/94

SUPERSEDES: 8/12/93

APPROVED:

PURPOSE

The Washington State Investment Board (SIB) has contracted with several managers using various styles to invest money for SIB retirement funds. SIB is required to monitor these managers as part of its fiduciary role as trustee. To evaluate the managers, staff monitors the specific areas of performance, investment characteristics, and operations, which include:

1. Performance

2. Style Integrity

3. Organization

4. Compliance

5. Client Service

The purpose of this policy is to establish *general* guidelines for monitoring and evaluating the investment managers' effectiveness, to identify potential issues and to provide a structure for the Board to employ when making decisions. Experience shows that, although concerns with managers' effectiveness can be divided into the five categories listed above, each manager situation is unique and must be thoroughly analyzed on an individual basis before action is taken. In addition, trends will become increasingly important over time in the evaluation of a manager's performance.

POLICY

The Public Markets Equity - Retirement Funds Policy, as adopted by the Board in June 1994, states that the equity segment of the portfolio is to be managed to achieve the highest return possible consistent with the desire to control asset volatility. To achieve this goal, the general strategy specifies that:

1. Passive index funds will be used in markets that are generally efficient. The structure should provide diversified market exposure while controlling risk and minimizing cost.

2. Active structured and specialty managers will be used in markets that are less efficient. The structure should actively seek to enhance returns while managing style risk.

Domestic Equity

The Board has structured the domestic equity portfolio to capture the broad market characteristics as measured by the Wilshire 5000 Index. The largest 500 capitalized companies represent about 70% of the Index and are believed to be priced efficiently most of the time. Consequently, to control costs, the Board has hired one manager to invest the bulk of the fund's large company stock investments passively to the S&P 500 Index. Additional managers have been hired to "enhance" the returns over the S&P 500 index.

The approximately 30% remaining of the Wilshire 5000 Index is represented by small-/mid-cap companies. About half of this equity segment is indexed. However, some opportunities for active management may exist due to inefficiencies in the markets for small companies. The markets are less efficient because the securities are not closely followed by financial analysts. Consequently, the other half is managed by advisors who specialize in research and investing in smaller companies that may be undervalued and/or possess growth potential.

International Equity

International markets are considered less efficient than the U.S. domestic markets and generally present an opportunity to enhance returns within the risk-controlled environment established by SIB. Therefore, approximately two-thirds of the core international assets are actively managed with specific regional equity mandates for Europe and the Pacific Basin, while one-third is indexed to the Morgan Stanley Capital International Europe, Australia, Far East (MSCI, EAFE) countries. The Board has targeted the total international equity portfolio to exceed the SIB normal benchmark composed of 50% MSCI EAFE-Europe, 35% MSCI EAFE-Japan, and 15% MSCI EAFE-Pacific Basin, excluding Japan. Currently, the noncore segment of the international portfolio consists of a global mandate investing in stocks, bonds, or cash. In the future, components of non-core may include emerging markets or currency management, if so approved by the Board.

PROCEDURE

1. Establish Guidelines

All managers, both domestic and international, are given discretion over the selection of individual securities for the portfolio. SIB staff broadly discusses strategies, industry developments, and security selection with the managers, but does not direct or specifically approve individual transactions in the portfolios or impose restrictions on investing except for those stated by contractual agreement or by law. Each manager agreement includes investment guidelines and policies, which specify return/risk expectations and investment restrictions.

2. Periodic Manager Reporting

As part of the monitoring process, SIB requires the managers to submit reports—monthly, quarterly, and annually. Staff collects and analyzes the data and disseminates periodic summary reports to senior management and the Board.

3. Staff Review/Analysis Contact

Although staff collects and analyzes many quantifiable details, a portion of the manager' evaluation is subjective and qualitative. Frequent contact with the managers is one of the most valuable tools staff uses in monitoring the managers.

4. Monitoring Criteria

This section outlines the five critical areas in which SIB monitors its managers: performance, style, organization, compliance, and client service.

A. *Performance:* The monitoring of performance is of primary importance in establishing the manager's "value added" to the overall fund. At least quarterly, each manager's returns (net of fees) are compared to the benchmark returns. From time to time, every manager experiences negative performance relative to the benchmark. The SIB focuses on trends and the long-term performance of the investment manager. Contracts are executed for three years with two annual renewal options which allows the manager to be evaluated over a full market cycle. Staff monitors the external managers' performance for a minimum period of four quarters, from inception, to establish an adequate track record for performance evaluation.

On a quarterly basis, SIB staff, consultant, and/or custodian prepares an in-depth performance evaluation on each manager, which is presented to the Board. The quarterly reports will include manager strategy, current market value, performance results, benchmark comparison, Sharpe ratios, fees, transaction costs, and significant events. The reports will rank the managers against one another on performance. In addition, each manager's historical performance will be graphically depicted against their established benchmark and a peer universe comprised of managers of a similar style. Any external manager experiencing negative deviations from their benchmark will be monitored in more detail to provide greater insight into the causes of the poor performance.

Transaction costs (e.g., commissions and the market impact of trading) are an integral part of a manager's performance. With the aid of an outside vendor specializing in transaction cost measuring and monitoring, the SIB will review and evaluate the managers' effectiveness in this area. Any external manager experiencing excessive turnover and/or transaction costs will be monitored in more detail to evaluate the impact of the increased transaction costs.

Another method to evaluate returns is the use of performance attribution analysis, which differentiates the source of returns (selection, weighting, and reallocation) for portfolios and benchmarks. Attribution explains what "bets" the external managers make that add (or diminish) value of the portfolios. At least annually, the staff will analyze various performance attribution statistics on each of the external managers.

B. *Style Definition:* At least annually, each manager's style will be identified, defined, and analyzed by SIB investment staff to insure the manager continues to invest the portfolio in the style for which they were originally hired. The annual review also allows SIB to confirm that the managers' roles continue to fit into the total fund equity structure.

The definition of managers' styles consists of analyzing several portfolio characteristics. Strong deviations in portfolio characteristics from that specified in the contract might infer a change of investment style.

Investment staff also conducts statistical analysis correlating each manager's returns against their benchmark, in addition to one another. Managers who have low correlations of returns amongst themselves can be a good way to structure a well diversified portfolio.

C. *Organization:* Contact between SIB and its external managers allows the external managers to understand how they integrate with SIB goals and objectives. Frequent contact can forewarn the investment staff of any potential problems. Major changes in the organization or rapid growth within the firm may indicate problems. Therefore, an annual update of each manager's organization and assets under management is requested by SIB investment staff.

- *Structure:* As part of the response to the Request for Proposal (RFP), investment managers provide an organizational structure chart and resumés of the key personnel working on the SIB account. This information provides staff with the initial structure of the firm when hired.

All organizations evolve over time; therefore, staff asks the investment managers to update the organizational structures of their firms at least annually. In addition, the contract requires the manager to notify SIB immediately if any major personnel changes occur in the organization. These types of changes include (1) staff and management additions or resignations, (2) reorganizations that remove current personnel from SIB account, or (3) ownership restructuring.

- *Account Universe:* In addition to the investment manager's organizational structure, staff reviews the manager's source of revenue, the total assets under management, and the total assets managed in the subject product. Staff also monitors the number, name, and asset value of client relationships which have been added or terminated in the past three years. This information is provided at contract inception and staff requests an update on an annual basis.

Staff analyzes SIB's account size in relation to the investment manager's assets in the subject product. When this percent exceeds 40%, staff will monitor the account more closely and may recommend a reduction in the account size.

D. Compliance: All managers must conform with various state and federal securities laws and specific reporting requirements of SIB. The following paragraphs outline SIB contractual requirements and how staff monitors the managers to ensure that their portfolios conform to those requirements.

• *Investment Guidelines:* Each contract specifies which investment vehicles a manager is authorized to use. SIB delineates between "domestic" and "international" securities. The contract also specifies in which of the following markets a manager is authorized to transact—equity, fixed income, cash, futures. Within a market, a manager could be limited by company characteristics (e.g., small capitalization companies only, value or growth orientation). SIB staff performs ongoing review of the transactions incurred by the manager and the assets held in each manager's portfolio to ensure compliance of the contract agreement.

• *Reconciliation:* Each month, the manager is required to certify that the portfolio market values and performance data are reconciled with the Master Custodian. Monthly reconciliation reduces the possibility of major discrepancies occurring when evaluating the manager's performance or verifying fee invoices.

• *Fee Billing:* The Board shall pay the investment manager a fee computed in accordance with the contract agreement for the services rendered. The investment manager shall submit each bill, which includes documentation of all values and the fee calculation to the Board. In the event of any discrepancy, the value as determined by SIB will prevail. The values used in the billing process will be verified and the calculation checked prior to approval for payment.

• *Proxy Issues:* In accordance with the investment management contracts, the Board reserves the right to vote all proxy issues. The Board may delegate proxy voting to managers of commingled funds or international portfolios.

- *Gratuities:* The managers are required to report to SIB any contributions they make or gratuities they provide to Washington political figures, SIB Board members, management, or staff. Where applicable, reporting requirements will comply with state law and Code of Conduct policy.

- *Reporting Requirements:* Managers are required to submit reports and documents in a timely manner. SIB staff may delay the processing of any fee billing if a manager fails to submit the appropriate reports.

- *Commissions:* Consistent with SIB policy 2.05.400 and the broad objectives, the SIB may request a manager to direct brokerage commissions for the Board, through SIB-specified broker firms. Directed commissions may be used to pay for investment services and products. When such transactions occur, summary reports of the trading activity will be required from the manager and the broker.

E. ***Client Service:*** The investment staff meets with each manager at least two times per year to review performance, style, organization structure, compliance, and client service. In addition, securities markets and managers' strategies are discussed and the meeting is often a forum to exchange ideas on new investment methods or concepts.

Augmenting the semiannual reviews is the day-to-day communication with the external manager via telephone and facsimile. Staff serves as a client liaison between SIB and the investment manager to handle a variety of issues that arise.

Managing an account for SIB requires attention to portfolio guidelines and reporting deadlines. In addition to routine reporting requirements, SIB often makes special requests to survey managers or analyze program efficiency. SIB provides timeframes for completion of all requests and expects the information to be disseminated in a timely and professional manner. Annually, SIB staff provides feedback to managers regarding the quality of their client service.

5. Manager Contract Review

A. *Preliminary Review:* This section defines the criteria used as monitoring guidelines—what constitutes inadequate performance, adherence to style, stable organizational structure, total assets under management, adequate compliance, and client servicing. This section also explains which actions are taken when managers do not meet SIB's expectations.

SIB is constantly reviewing the quality of the relationship with its managers by telephone, periodic meetings at SIB headquarters, and monthly, quarterly, and annual reporting. At times, it is necessary to call a manager's attention to certain areas which need improvement. As discussed before, monitoring is not just a quantitative exercise of performance measurement, but also considers qualitative and subjective aspects.

Outlined below are three levels in the manager contract review: Watchlist, Probation, and Dismissal. Although great effort has been taken to establish specific timeframes and level of underperformance, SIB knows from experience that each situation that is a potential for contract review is unique. Contract review may occur if a manager experiences consecutive quarters of underperformance against the agreed upon benchmark or the Sharpe ratio. The specific guidelines, especially for performance and related issues, are dependent upon the type of manager and the style/strategy employed. For example, *passive index portfolios* replicate or represent a stratified sample of the agreed upon index and should track the index closely. Because of the efficiency of markets, the returns of domestic index portfolios should track the specified index closer than the returns of international index portfolios would be expected to track their index. Higher returns, but with more volatility, are anticipated in actively managed portfolios versus passive portfolios. The minimum long-term objective for SIB's *actively-managed domestic portfolios* is an excess return over the specified benchmark of 100 basis points for enhanced indexers and an excess return of 200 basis points for active small-, mid-, and large-cap portfolios.

The descriptions of Watchlist, Probation, and Dismissal should be viewed as the general conditions that would place a manager on contract review. Prior to a manager being placed on contract review, several steps are taken.

• *Discussions with the Manager:* Before a firm is recommended for either level of the contract review (Watchlist or Probation), staff may request that the pension consultant provide input to the process. Discussions with the manager may be written or verbal (in a meeting or via telephone). Each manager situation is individually reviewed and analyzed by staff and the pension consultant.

• *Analysis:* The following list specifies the numerous aspects related to performance that staff may analyze before a manager is recommended for contract review.

Evaluate the manager's performance on the SIB portfolio:

- To determine that the minimum objective of excess return over the benchmark is met, analyze the active domestic manager's performance from inception for four consecutive quarters.

- Relative to the agreed upon benchmark over time.

- Relative to other SIB managers, managers of the same strategy/style, other manager universes, or a style index.

- Relative to other accounts that the manager has under management.

- Compare total returns vs. equity-only returns to identify the effect of cash drag on the portfolio.

- Analyze trends of the manager's performance.

- Analyze how the returns were generated (Performance Attribution) and the level of risk taken (Sharpe Analysis).

- Analyze the relation of the manager's portfolio to other SIB portfolios and the total SIB fund.

- Analyze the relationship of manager's performance to style, structural, and investment characteristics over time.

Review the manager's contractual compliance and organizational structure.

Review the manager's guidelines, strategy, and style, especially the buy/sell disciplines.

Analyze the manager's turnover rate and execution costs.

Compare the portfolio market value to the funded level.

Evaluate the stability of personnel.

• *Meeting:* As needed, face-to-face meetings may be scheduled with staff, the manager, and pension consultant to discuss the concerns related to the account.

• *Review/Decision:* After a thorough review is conducted, a manager may be a candidate for Watchlist or Probation. Staff may determine when it is appropriate to place a manager on Watchlist and then report the action to the Committee/Board. Staff and/or the pension consultant will recommend to the Committee/Board those managers who are candidates for Probation. The Committee/Board then approves or disapproves the recommendation for action.

• *Statement of Concerns:* SIB staff will notify the manager of SIB's decision to place the firm on Watchlist or Probation. A Statement of Concerns will outline in writing the manager's deficiencies and areas which need improvement.

• *Manager's Response:* The manager will be asked to provide a written response to the Statement of Concerns. The response should include an explanation of the issues (for example, possible reasons for underperformance), and the proposed action(s) to resolve the issues.

• *Plan of Action:* The manager's response will provide a basis for a meeting or conference-call in which SIB staff, the manager, and the pension consultant will collectively draft a Plan of Action. The Plan will designate (1) the timeframe for the Contract Review, (2) what additional information the manager will provide SIB, and (3) the specific steps to be followed to correct the deficiency.

B. *Watchlist:* The following conditions are the guidelines for identifying managers who are potential candidates for Watchlist. Watchlist denotes an increased level of concern, but does not indicate major deficiencies. Watchlist establishes a period to assess the capabilities and quality of the manager's investment skill and operations. Staff may place a firm on Watchlist and report this action at the next meeting of the Committee/Board.

1. CONDITION: *The manager is underperforming.*

Passive index managers—Table 1 summarizes the performance guidelines (returns, net of fees) established for the passive money management firms. Since index managers are expected to track closely to the specified benchmark, the actual performance criteria for Watchlist and Probation are the same: the annualized return of the domestic S&P index portfolio should track within 5 basis points of the benchmark return, the domestic extended markets portfolio within 50 to 75 basis points, and the international portfolio within 25 basis points of their specified benchmark return. Prolonged negative tracking error greater than the specified criteria and/or noncompliance with other conditions could warrant probation.

Enhanced index managers—As shown in Table 2, the guidelines for Watchlist are: over a period of two consecutive quarters, the manager's cumulative portfolio returns since inception are below the cumulative benchmark returns in the rage of 50 to 200 basis points. A comparable value relative ratio (VRR) since inception is between 97% and 99%.

Active, nonindexed managers—Over a period of two consecutive quarters, the manager's cumulative benchmark returns are in a range of 150 to 350 basis points. A comparable value relative ratio since inception is between 95% and 97%. Watchlist may also be appropriate during the initial four quarters of asset management, if the manager's performance is 100 to 200 basis points below the benchmark.

Table 2 summarizes suitable guidelines for evaluating the enhanced index managers and active managers' underperformance. The table depicts three factors to measure underperformance versus both long-term (LT) and short-term (ST) benchmarks: (1) the value relative ratio, (2) the cumulative difference since inception of linked returns of the portfolio, and (3) the Sharpe ratio, which analyzes return per unit of risk. Performance is measured and evaluated since inception of the account, but SIB's focus is long-term; therefore, recommendations for watchlist or probation generally are not taken until the first 12 months.

The value relative ratio (VRR) relates the cumulative portfolio value as a percentage of the cumulative benchmark value at a comparable point in time. When the returns of the benchmark and the portfolio are equal, the ratio is 1.00 (one). A VRR of approximately 1.00 (one) is acceptable for an index manager, whose strategy is to track the benchmark. At a ratio of 1.00 (one), an active manager is not adding value over an indexed strategy. When the portfolio return is below (above) the benchmark, the ratio is less (greater) than 1.00 (one).

2. **CONDITION:** *The organization incurs a minor change— marketing or support personnel on the SIB account leave the firm or a reorganization occurs that does not involve key personnel working on the SIB portfolio.*

As Watchlist implies, SIB will observe a firm that has undergone personnel changes to verify that the manager continues to efficiently run its operations with personnel available.

TABLE 1. INDEXED PORTFOLIOS
Measurement of Underperformance

	ANNUALIZED RETURNS (BP BELOW BENCHMARK)	NUMBER OF CONSECUTIVE QUARTERS
DOMESTIC:		
S&P Index	5 bp	4
EXTENDED MARKET:		
ST (< 3 years)	75 bp	4
LT (3 years +)	50 bp	4
INTERNATIONAL:		
Non-U.S. Country Index Funds	25 bp	4

3. **CONDITION:** *Partial Compliance with Specified Directives. Examples include: investment guidelines, directed commission goals, reporting deadlines. Managers are expected to comply with all laws, regulations, and standards of conduct related to the securities/investment industry. The specifics surrounding each compliance issue will determine whether or not the manager is included on the Watchlist.*

If the manager cannot comply with guidelines, directed commission goals, or reporting deadlines, SIB should be given prior notification, a justification, and timeframe for the manager's special needs. In some cases, a variance may be allowed for such directives.

When managers are not in compliance with all monthly reporting requirements, they are first contacted by the staff. If the manager's reports are consistently delinquent, the payment of fees may be delayed.

• *Unauthorized Investments:* If a manager purchases unauthorized investments, leverages the account, or invests in unauthorized countries, the securities must be liquidated according to the guidelines established by the staff. Managers are responsible to reimburse SIB for any losses that may occur in the liquidation of an unauthorized purchase.

TABLE 2. ACTIVELY MANAGED PORTFOLIOS

Measurement of Underperformance

	VALUE RELATIVE RATIO	CUMULATIVE LINKED RETURNS (bp below benchmark)	SHARPE RATIO (% below)	NUMBER OF CONSECUTIVE QUARTERS
ENHANCED INDEX PORTFOLIOS:				
Watchlist	99%	50 - 200	30%	Initial 4 quarters or 2 consecutive quarters after first year
Probation	97%	150-350	30%	2
ACTIVELY MANAGED PORTFOLIOS *(Domestic and International):*				
Watchlist		100-200bp		Initial 4 Quarters
Watchlist	97%	150-350 bp	30%	2
Probation	95%	300-600 bp	30%	2

Cumulative Linked Returns: Monthly returns linked since inception (not annualized) for comparison of portfolio and benchmark performance.

Value Relative Ratio (VRR): Cumulative linked portfolio value (Rp) as a percentage of cumulative linked benchmark (Rb) value. when Rp = Rb, VRR = 100%.

Sharpe Ratio: Value added by manager per unit of risk.

Note: The values stated for the VRR and Sharpe ratios are targets; staff will analyze manager's performance within ranges of these criteria.

- *Commissions:* Managers may be asked to direct commissions to specified brokers or types of brokers (minority/women-owned). If the firm is not in compliance with the allocation to directed commissions, the quota may be increased to recapture the previously forfeited commissions.

- *Assets under Management:* Becoming a major portion of a manager's business may not be beneficial to the client or the manager. The size of the SIB portfolio in relation to the manager's assets under management is affected by market conditions, the growth of the SIB account relative to other accounts, and the addition or termination of client relationships. Guidelines for the appropriate size of the SIB portfolio are 25% or less of the manager's total assets and 40% or less of the manager's subject product.

4. **CONDITION:** *Client service has not been reasonable, professional, or timely.*

Although SIB outlines the deadlines for its reporting requirements and special projects, a great deal of time may be spent reminding managers of timeframes and collecting past due data. Deadlines are established so that SIB staff and consultants can report punctually on the External Manager Program to the Public Markets Committee or Board. Also, monthly performance and market value reconciliation data is necessary for the payment of invoices for investment services rendered. Therefore, prompt submission of data benefits the managers directly.

It is estimated that managers on the Watchlist for performance-related issues or organizational changes would remain on the list for a minimum of two quarters. This timeframe helps to insure that the issue is resolved for the longer term. Managers with partial compliance or poor client service should remedy the situation immediately (in one quarter at a maximum). Managers who do not correct the outstanding issues in a timely manner could be advanced to a higher level of contract review.

C. *Probation:* Probation is the second level of contract review and indicates a level of serious deficiency. The Public Markets Committee or Board will determine when a manager is placed on or taken off probation. Probation is stipulated for managers who have one of the following deficiencies:

1. **CONDITION:** *A manager is significantly underperforming.* (Refer to Tables 1 and 2.)

   Passive Index Managers: Index managers are expected to track closely to the specified benchmark. The performance criteria for Watchlist and Probation are the same.

   Enhanced Index Managers: Over a period of two consecutive quarters, the manager's cumulative portfolio returns since inception are below the cumulative benchmark returns in the range of 150 to 350 basis points. A comparable value relative ratio since inception is below 97%.

   Active, nonindexed managers: Over a period of two consecutive quarters, the manager's cumulative portfolio returns since inception are below the cumulative benchmark returns in the range of 300 to 600 basis points. A comparable value relative ratio since inception is below 95%.

2. **CONDITION:** *The manager deviates from the style category. Manager's portfolio characteristics are significantly different from their stated style.*

   Since style and performance are closely related, a review similar to that specified for underperformance under Watchlist would be analyzed if a manager was possibly deviating from his style. Staff review would emphasize the analysis related to (1) comparison with style and portfolio guidelines/characteristics profile, (2) performance attribution, (3) review of returns, (4) comparison against a style or normal benchmark, and/or (5) statistical/correlation analysis.

   It is important to verify that a manager maintains style integrity throughout all market cycles. Below-market performance can be acceptable if the manager is following the style, but the style is out of favor. At least once a year, SIB staff performs an in-depth analysis of the style integrity of its managers.

Another method of analyzing manager's adherence to the strategy plots the manager's style over time. For example, a graph of capitalization (representing large to small) versus growth/value characteristics will visually demonstrate shifts in style over time.

3. **CONDITION:** *The firm incurs a significant change in organization.*

- *New Ownership:* A manager may be placed on probation if the firm's ownership changes. The specific situation will be reviewed to analyze the degree of impact the new ownership has on the investment manager. The type of new ownership situation which causes SIB less concern is when the investment management team handling the SIB account is left intact and fairly autonomous. When people key to the SIB portfolio leave or are transferred off the account, probation is appropriate.

  Probation is not an indication of SIB's dissatisfaction with the organization change, but that staff desires closer contact with the firm and to be well-informed regarding the impact the new ownership has on the organization and management.

- *Turnover:* Although personnel in the investment business often have opportunities to advance their careers with other firms, significant turnover in top management, portfolio managers, research, or trading staff may be of concern in a long-term client relationship. Turnover involving key personnel working on the SIB account is a cause for probation.

- *Reorganization:* Similar to the issues with turnover, reorganizations can disassemble the investment team hired for management of the SIB account. The personnel, although still with the firm, may no longer be directly responsible for managing the SIB portfolio.

  Organizational transformations may represent favorable changes in the management of the SIB account, but they can also signal management deterioration or hasty growth in the firm. In any case, staff desires a proactive approach and close communication with the firm. Therefore, probation indicates a cautious and observant relationship with the manager. Comparisons of performance, style characteristics, compliance, and client servicing before and after the ownership/personnel change can help identify potential problems with the account.

4. **CONDITION:** *The manager is not in full compliance.*

- *Professional Conduct:* If the manager does not comply with the securities laws, industry regulations, professional conduct standards, or contractual agreements, probation will be invoked. The possibility of immediate dismissal is dependent on the circumstances.

- *Compliance with Specific Directives:* If a manager continues noncompliance with investment guidelines, commission goals, or reporting deadlines, probation can be considered.

D. *Removal From Contract Review:* Managers who show indications of an improved situation may be moved to the Watchlist (from the probation status) or may be removed totally from the Contract Review process.

After the manager rectifies all deficiencies outlined in the Plan of Action and has continued success in all other areas of the relationship, staff may recommend to the Public Markets Committee or Board that an investment management firm be removed from Contract Review.

- *Improved Performance:* The specific improvement will be specified in the Plan of Action and is dependent on the manager's risk profile and style. For example, a manager may be removed from Contract Review if the firm achieves improved performance for at least two consecutive quarters. If the manager is on Probation, a significant upward trend in performance could move the manager off Probation and onto the Watchlist.

- *Style Characteristics:* The manager restores style elements and portfolio characteristics originally established in the contract and continues to maintain those characteristics in the portfolio management process.

- *Organizational Structure:* The manager must demonstrate that organization changes have not adversely affected the operation and performance of SIB's portfolio.

- *Fully Meet All Compliance Requirements/Improved Client Service:* The manager must conduct all business in a professional manner, comply with all laws, complete deficient reporting requirements, and reconcile all accounting statements.

E. Persistent Deficiencies: If, in a timely manner (typically one year), the manager does not correct all the deficiencies as outlined in the Plan of Action, staff and/or the pension consultant will prepare a special report to the Public Markets Committee or Board on the manager's progress. After reviewing the situation, the following actions may be taken:

- Continue probation
- Reduce the manager's assets under management
- Review investment guidelines
- Renegotiate fees
- Dismiss the manager

If it is in the best interest of the Fund, probation may be continued beyond the one-year period. Reasons for prolonged probation include (1) manager is making reasonable progress, but has not totally resolved all deficiencies, (2) additional issues developed during the probation period, (3) high cost or unfavorable market conditions for immediate restructuring of the portfolio's assets.

Moderate actions might include partial reallocation of the manager's assets or a renegotiation of the manager's fees. Although the ultimate action is dismissal, this action should be thoroughly analyzed before making the final decision.

F. *Dismissal:* Prior to making the final decision to dismiss a firm, the Public Markets Committee or Board may invite the manager to make a presentation at its monthly or a special meeting. When the manager has significantly underperformed both the short-term benchmark and the long-term benchmark as indicated under conditions of probation, staff may recommend dismissal to the Public Markets Committee/Board. Before a manager is officially dismissed, staff analyzes how to transition the assets effected by the termination. Staff establishes a plan of action for managing (internally, externally, or in combination) or liqui-dating the assets.

Upon Board approval (or in an emergency, the Executive Director) the investment manager and custodian will be formally notified of termination. The method of notification will include communication by telephone and a fax of the written formal notification, followed by a certified letter of formal termination.

Upon notice of termination, the SIB will inform the investment manager when to cease all trading and how to conduct final activities with the SIB, custodian bank, and other pertinent parties.

Upon the decision to terminate, SIB's internal operations per-sonnel—Deputy Director for Operations, Contracts Specialist, Controller, and Business Manager—are notified of the action. All outstanding issues with the master custodian, brokers, pension consultant(s), or other parties and the investment manager are to be resolved before the conclusion of the contract. To solve any discrepancies, funds may be withheld from the last quarterly fee invoice.

SUMMARY

This report explains the process and guidelines used by staff to judge the quality of external investment management and outlines the reports generated during the monitoring process. Considering both the objective and subjective aspects of the monitoring process, staff analyzes five main categories to evaluate the managers: performance, style integrity, organizational structure, contractual compliance, and client service.

Using the five categories to gauge the quality of the manager's accomplishments, the report also defines inadequate service on the SIB portfolio and explains what actions are taken when managers do not meet SIB's expectations. Three levels of Contract Review are outlined: Watchlist, Probation, and Dismissal. Although general conditions are profiled in the report which would activate the Contract Review, the conditions which remove a manager from the Contract Review or conditions which constitute reasons for Dismissal also are specified. Each Contract Review situation is evaluated individually by staff and the pension consultant. While staff may place a firm on Watchlist and report to the Public Markets Committee or Board, action to place a manager on Probation will be recommended by staff and decided by the Public Markets Committee or Board.

SIB's staff continues to identify improved methods of monitoring performance, attribution, and style, as well as tools for developing the appropriate mix of managers and styles. Staff is in contact not only with the external managers but also with consultants and other pension fund personnel who monitor managers. The staff considers monitoring a continual process to develop, refine, and incorporate new analytical techniques for the program.

INDEX